FATAL FRIENDSHIP

The Death of Helen Richey
and the
Strange Disappearance of Amelia Earhart

Andrea Niapas

with
David K. Bowman

First printing, July 2014

This edition was printed by Grelin Press
P.O. Box 367, New Kensington, PA 15068
(724) 334-8240   grelinpress@aol.com

Table of Contents

Acknowledgments

Ms. Geraldine Jurann who throughout the years would send me articles on Helen Richey's career, which got me started on my journey to bring this remarkable pilot to life. I will always be grateful for Gerry's support.

John Sharbaugh, with his computer expertise, made the editing process of this book a whole lot easier.

A special thank you to David K. Bowman for his input on the importance those Itasca transmissions were in the grand scheme of the rescue.

Louise Foudray, the honorary host of the Amelia Earhart Birthplace, who has welcome visitors, students, and researchers to the museum for nearly thirty years.

The McKeesport Heritage Center and, especially, my go-to person Gail Waite who always had time to look up information I needed while compiling this book.

Amy Gamble-Lannan, for her priceless interviews, letters, and photos.

Betty Shaw-Gamble and Guy P. Gamble, for their eyewitness accounts of Amelia Earhart's visits to the Richey home in McKeesport, PA.

Brooke Gamble, for her assistance in obtaining Helen Richey's A. T. A. records.

Guy (Tracy) Gamble for his support.

Richard Poad, Chairman of the Maidenhead Heritage Centre in the United Kingdom, for his generous help with my research.

So Long, Old Friend

The gypsy wind,
It called your name,
No time to say goodbye.
You left us here alone, old friend,
To take your final ride.

The world, it couldn't tame your soul,
You lived your life with pride.
Now you soar free-like an eagle,
You're on your final ride.

Your memory won't fade, old friend,
We'll hold you deep inside.
We'd come with you if we could,
Upon your final ride.

It's time to say so long, old friend,
As you take your final ride.
We'll keep you with us in our hearts,
If not riding by our side.

--Anonymous

Chapter 1

Awaiting Word

By mid-June 1937 Helen decided to return to her hometown of McKeesport, Pennsylvania to attend the wedding of her niece Amy. Excited to see family and friends Helen was also deeply concerned with the last leg of Amelia Earhart and Fred Noonan's World Flight. Part of her wished to stay in California so she could greet them upon their return, but she would feel guilty if she didn't appear at her cousin's wedding. After all, Helen hadn't been back to visit her family for two years. Her air marking schedule kept her based in California, conducting flights throughout the West Coast states. Now that her parents were getting older, she felt a yearning to return. Before leaving California she loaded a few bushels of freshly picked oranges on her plane—a real treat her mother and sister loved to serve with breakfast.

No trip back East went unplanned without a stop at the Happy Bottom Riding Club which was owned and operated by fellow pilot Pancho Barnes. It was legendary for its big meals, lots of liquor, and live dance bands. The ranch was tucked away in the desert brush of Palm Springs. After catching up on old times with Pancho and friends, Helen turned in to get an early start the next morning.

After reviewing her map, listening to the weather report on the radio, and extending thanks to Pancho for the layover, Helen was set for take-off. The weather conditions stayed in the good range all day. Making a few fuel stops left her just enough day light to reach the Ohio boarder.

Cleveland, Ohio and Peggy Rex was her next destination along her route to Pennsylvania. Peggy Rex was known to all the pilots as 'Cleveland's First Lady of Aviation.' For years Peggy would open her home to any flyers going east that needed a layover spot. During the Cleveland National Air Races, all participants were showered with her hospitality from the moment they touched down on the field until final take off. She would arrange to have cars lined up to transfer the gals to her home and homes of the committee women. Awaiting those tired dust-blown pilots were refreshments, hot bubble baths, home-cooked meals, entertainment, soft beds, and, most of all, comradeship. Having fond memories of past good times, Helen looked forward to dropping in to say hello, and her visit quickly turned into a delicious meal and hours of conversation. By now the sun had gone down, so Helen decided to take Peggy up on her offer to layover. At the crack of dawn Helen was awaken to the smell of bacon and eggs. Thanking Peggy and promising to visit again, Helen caught a taxi to the airfield.

It was only a three hour flight to Bettis field located up the hill from McKeesport, Pennsylvania. Approaching the landing field, Helen's descent was rocky. The winds already picked up during morning hours. To compensate she had to apply more control to the rudder. As she reduced the plane's altitude, she could ease up on the rudder. It was all a balancing act until the wheels touched down on the field. By now she could make out the people on the ground as the excitement of landing the plane after her cross county excursion was coming to an end. Nothing she was experiencing, though, could compare to what Amelia and Fred were probably enduring as they flew over South American, Africa, India, and by now the Far East. As she crossed states they were crossing continents.

When it came to them flying over countries in the Far East, Helen felt the Japanese had to be aware of every mile the Electra flew over as well as its probable destination. The Japanese read American newspapers, and listened to broadcasts over American radio stations across the United States and Hawaii. Surely they were following the World Flight news from day one. Perhaps even before. After all, the route was designed to fly over the Pacific Ocean on the original attempt in March and now in July. There was no way that last leg of the flight could be excluded from the route. It was a dangerous risk. Did Amelia and Fred understand the consequences if anything should go wrong? Were they briefed at all?

By now Helen had touched down on the air field, slowly driving the plane up to the nearest hanger to park it. Once it came to a complete stop she cut the engine.

As she was gathering up her purse, three mechanics ran up to the plane carrying a roster. After completing all the forms, she handed the roaster and keys to the mechanic in charge. "See you in a few days we'll have your plane fueled and ready for you, Miss Richey!" Thanking him for helping her unload the baskets of oranges, she tossed a few to him and his buddies.

Lucille Gamble (her older sister) had just pulled up her car honking the horn to get Helen's attention. "I heard you were in town kid. Need a ride"?

As they greeted one another with hugs Helen wanted to hear all the details of Amy's wedding as well as the latest news around McKeesport. But first and foremost was a stop at Minerva's bakery for several dozens of their famous cinnamon rolls. Lucille assured Helen that she had placed the order yesterday knowing how much she craved the treat with a cup of Eight O'Clock coffee. Helen tossed her suitcase in the backseat of the car with the baskets of oranges. Off they drove leaving behind a cloud of dust.

Down the hill and over the Dravosburg Bridge they went, slowing while rounding a sharp curve leading down 5th Avenue. After picking up the goodies at Minerva's, they drove to the Richey home on Jenny Lind Street. Lucille pulled the car up to the curb in front of the Richey residence. It was a large three story, white wood frame house, surrounded by trees, with a barn in the backyard. Mr. and Mrs. Richey, with Helen's other brothers, were sitting on the wraparound porch. Helen was the youngest of the Richey siblings and the only one who took to flying plane. The others chose grounded careers in education, banking, and medicine. They spent the remainder of the afternoon catching up on old times.

The next day was full of trying on dresses at Cox's and J.C. Penney's, shoes at Katzman's, followed by lunch at Isaly's. They had the best chipped ham sandwiches with Heinz brown mustard.

After lunch they wondered over to the DeLuxe Beauty Shoppe, which was Helen's favorite beauty shop since her high school days. Bonnie, the owner, could cut and perm hair better than any hair expert in all of Pittsburgh according to Helen.

Finally, after a long day of pampering and relaxation, they were ready to return home to get ready for Amy's wedding which was scheduled for 5:30 and followed by dinner. There Helen met Amy's future husband and all the members of the Lannan family.

As the wedding party slowly walked down the center of the church, Amy looked beautiful. Only seven years younger than Helen, they were like sisters, and she could be seen wiping away tears of joy. After the ceremony photos were taken, with Amy insisting one be taken with Helen. Then the wedding party went off to the Penn-McKee Hotel where a sit-down dinner reception was to take place.

With her glass in hand, Helen honored the bride and groom with a toast. The toasting was followed by a delicious dinner, drinks, cake, and dancing. As the evening was coming to an end, Amy was ready to toss her bouquet. Quickly all the single gals gather onto the dance floor as Amy send her beautiful Lilly of the Valley bouquet into the air. Everyone jumped up and down for it; Helen opened her arms and the bundle of flowers fell right into her hands. The Sammy Marlo band played on as Helen paraded around the dance floor laughing and waving the bouquet to the audience. Photographers were following her around and flash bulbs were going off left and right.

As the evening closed, the bride and groom rushed out the doors as guest threw handfuls of rice in their direction. Waving goodbye they drove off to begin their new life as husband and wife. Everyone headed back into the Penn-McKee for one more toast before they called it a night. Up Versailles Avenue the car went as Helen drove her mother and father home.

Early the next day, much to Helen's surprise, she received a phone call from her friend Bobby Myers back in California. He had promised her he would call if he heard anything on his ham radio pertaining to Amelia's flight. The call disturbed her because Bobby had over-heard a conversation between two men at the Bay Farm airport stating that they heard the Electra needed repairs during their layover in Lae, New Guinea. Noonan didn't want to take any chances departing from New Guinea if there were going to be any mechanical problems. They were now attempting not only the longest non-stop distance flight, but also the most dangerous. From the air, islands along their route were almost too tiny to see let alone trying to locate a spot to land the Electra if the need arose. Furthermore the Japanese army and navy canvassed the mandates regularly. With Howland Island their final destination, the plane's tanks had to hold as much fuel as they could. Those mandates were owned by the Japanese and they were off limits!

Helen knew that no matter what she told Bobby, he would worry about Amelia and Fred. So the only thing that came to her mind was to tell him to continue to listen for any new developments. Letting him know she was on her way back to California assured him he wasn't alone. Bobby was fifteen years old, still a kid who thought the world of Amelia Earhart.

As the hours ticked away Helen knew Amelia and Fred's lives were on the line. All she could think about was to return to California as soon as possible, just in case the worst should happen. She quickly packed up her suitcase and proceeded downstairs, placing it near the door. Next a call to Bettis field to have her plane fueled. It was time for her to get back to California.

Mr. and Mrs. Richey were still in the kitchen as Helen entered. Surprised at Helen's announcement to cut her visit short, they understood her concern. Mrs. Richey packed a few sandwiches, a piece of chocolate cake, and a thermos full of coffee to hold Helen over during her flight. After all the goodbyes, Dr. Richey drove her to airfield. Within twenty-five minutes Helen was airborne in a westward direction.

Chapter 2

Golden Girls

Once Helen reached the altitude needed to maintain a smooth flowing flight, she settled in for the long trip back to the West Coast. All the earthly ties of everyday life seemed as if they were a million miles away. The familiar sound of wind flowing through the cracks around the door frame as well as the hum of the engine relaxed her, and she let her thoughts pleasurably drift. Helen begin to think about what exactly got her so interested in flying in the first place.

One of Helen's enjoyments as a child growing up was reading. During summer vacations she would spend hot afternoons a few blocks from her home at the McKeesport library. The librarian would display reading books on the main floor. On a large wooden table sat dozens of books for young patrons to check out during the summer months. One particular book, with a bright red, orange, blue, and yellow colored hot air balloon on a cover, caught her attention. Titled *The Adventures of Frances Thibel*, the book drew Helen to it like a magnet. Gently picking the book up, she read a few sentences on the first page, the flipped through it from cover to cover. There was a picture of the hero in book, Frances Thibel standing inside of a large brown basket connected to a huge balloon. The balloon was suspended in air as it touched the white clouds beside it. People on the ground appeared tiny. With a smile on Helen's face she quickly closed the book and made her way to the librarian's desk to check out the book. She couldn't wait to get home to continue reading about Frances's adventures riding across the sky in a hot air balloon.

After dinner that evening when the Richeys gathered around in the living room, Helen asked if they would like to hear about a book she had read? They all watched as she held the book up in front of herself. She went on to explain about the adventures of the first female to fly in a hot air balloon in the year 1784. As Helen told the story, her family listened with delight. Mrs. Richey could tell her daughter had found a subject of great interest.

Week after week Helen would check out books about aviation from the library. She had certainly found her calling that summer of 1923. Just before it was time to begin the school year she asked her father to take her to visit Franklin, Pennsylvania. She wanted to see the spot where the 1883 altitude record was established by Mary Myers, the first female to solo in a hot air balloon. Little did Helen know that one day she too would break an altitude record of 18,000 feet.

During her teenage years she followed pilot Katherine Stinson's career. Each time articles would appear in the newspaper of Katherine's flights Helen would cut them out. Over the years she pasted them in a scrap book. Her dream was to one day visit the Stinson School of Flying located in San Antonio, Texas. What a thrill it would be to meet Katherine Stinson and her family. Because each member held pilot licenses, the Stinsons published their own magazine, listing numerous courses in the field of aeronautics. Within the pages of the magazine was a two-page application to attend the school. If only her parents would let her attend! Helen ripped out the application, hoping that one day she would be able to fill it out and send it in.

While other girls in the neighborhood Helen's age were painting their fingernails, listening to the radio, and going to parties, Helen was learning how to repair bicycles, her motorcycle, and car engines. Those activities didn't exactly sit well with her father. Dr. Richey wanted all his children to attend college and pursue careers in education, medicine, or business.

Helen's high school years were ending in 1927, and she made sure she participated in as many activities as possible. As a committee member she helped organize dances, the Pitt literary meet team, and working on the Yough-A-Mon yearbook. She was even the make-up artist for two plays: *The Ballet of the Nation's* and the last act of *Le Bourgeois Gentelhome*.

Helen kept her preparatory grades up so she could pass the entrance exams to attend Carnegie Technology in Pittsburgh, with a major in education to satisfy her father. She found the semester's work boring, but Sunday afternoon visits to Bettis airfield to watch the barnstormers spin and race across the sky kept her desire to fly alive and that soon became her top priority.

When Amelia Earhart became the first female pilot to fly across the Atlantic Ocean in 1928, the desire for adventure overpowered Helen's studies to become a teacher. More visits to the airfield, talking to the other pilots, and learning about what makes planes fly from the mechanics now convinced Helen to follow her heart. But how could she break the news to her parents? By now her brothers and sister had pleased their parents by settling into promising careers. Mrs. Richey, however, supported her daughter's drive to take flying lessons. After Helen passed her student pilots permit in 1930 than her pilot's license in 1931, it was Mrs. Richey who persuaded her husband to purchase Helen's first plane. Dr. Richey had to recognize that Helen wasn't going to settle into a classroom when she had her eyes on the sky.

Helen used the four-passenger Bird plane Dr. Richey purchased for her to fly charters and sightseeing trips from Pittsburgh to Philadelphia. The money she was paid covered the cost of fuel and enabled her to open a savings account. With her own plane she now joined the ranks of other Pittsburgh female pilots such as Louise Thaden, Helen MacCloskey, and Theresa James. At just twenty-two years of age Helen Richey had her own plane and was making a name for herself among the most popular record-breaking female aviators in the United States.

The first time she met Amelia Earhart was right after Amelia's 1928 Atlantic Ocean crossing. On a publicity tour arranged by her manager, George Putnam, Amelia visited numerous cities throughout the United States. Pittsburgh was one of them. Just as Amelia landed her light sport plane onto the muddy runway of Rogers Field in Fox Chapel, the wheels sunk into the mud. The landing gears snapped at the impact, causing additional damage to the propeller. Three of the airfield's mechanics came running over to assist.

Helen remembered riding her motorcycle to Roger Field hoping to see the plane and its famous pilot. That was the first time Helen set eyes on Amelia Earhart. Little did she know then how her life and Amelia's would become entwined.

By now Helen was passing over the state of Indiana. Continuing to fly on to California was out of the question.

She was hoping to make it to Kansas by dark. There she could sleep over, fuel up, and get an early start the next morning. Once landed, she taxied up to the hanger and turned off the engine. The airport was overrun with people. It was Saturday evening and folks were traveling in and out of the city, but that hardly seemed enough to cause the crowds.

Filling out forms for her plane to be serviced she asked what all the commotion was about? A passenger standing next to her in line handed her the July 3rd *Atchison Daily Globe* Saturday newspaper. The headline read: "Amelia's Voice Heard by Amateur Radio Operator . . . Plane Adrift at Sea. Former Atchison Girl and Companion Forced Down When Fuel is Exhausted on Perilous Flight." In shock, Helen sat down to read the article. Morning couldn't come soon enough. Grabbing a quick breakfast she rode over to the airfield to checkout out her plane, paid her bill, and waited for clearance to lift off.

She hadn't slept well the night before but she pushed on, knowing the rest of the trip would go fast because she had caught the tail wind. Conditions reminded her of the 1933 Endurance Race she and her good friend Frances Marsalis piloted together. It was sponsored by the manufacturers of Outdoor Girl cosmetics. Both gals took turns piloting the aircraft as they circled Miami, Florida. The race began December 20th and ended on the 30th, breaking the endurance record of 196 hours and five minutes set by Louise Thaden and Frances Marsalis in 1932. That race took place over Valley Stream, New York. Achieving that triumph was the turning point of Helen's future in aviation history. She left the ranks of amateur pilot to become a professional rising star. All of which was accomplished in just two years after securing a pilot's license. Many in the field agreed that Helen Richey was considered a natural-born pilot.

Like Amelia and others, one can never sit on her merits because there was always another pilot in hot pursuit. After all it cost money to fly: plane parts, maintenance, hanger rent, fuel, applications for races, food, lodging, and so forth must be paid in order to participate in races throughout the country. In the early 1930's pilots (both men and women) were trying to get their names out into the public eye. Their goal was to secure endorsements from oil companies, aircraft designers, and manufacturers. Not everyone was as lucky as Amelia to have a marketing agent in their corner. Therefore, entering races and breaking records in altitude and distance was the business Helen selected to establish her career. Along with the uncertainty of success came the real risks of aircrafts crashing due to weather conditions, pilot error, and mechanical fault.

Could this be what Amelia and Fred were now facing in the middle of the Pacific Ocean, she wondered? What went wrong? The more Helen focused on the uncertainties of their safety, the faster she pushed her plane. Her desire to land at Bay Farm airport and catch up with Bobby Myers was now consuming her. What did he hear? He promised Amelia that he would listen in on her radio calls. What did he hear?

The poor kid must be scared out of his mind at this point. Bobby was a loyal fan of Amelia's the entire time she and Fred were held up at Farm Bay while the Electra was being fixed. During the months of March, April, May, and June, Amelia confided in him. Helen remem-bered Amelia telling Bobby, "If anything goes wrong during the world flight please tell someone, your parents, a teacher just someone!" Right then and there it was all making sense to her. Helen made a promise to herself to get to the bottom of the mystery. Could Amelia and Fred be casualties of some sort of elaborate plan?

By now Helen had reached Colorado. In another three hours the San Francisco Golden Gate Bridge should be beneath her plane. The bridge reminded her of all the bridges that connected the communities to downtown Pittsburgh. Even in her hometown there were several bridges she had to fly over to get from McKeesport to Homestead and Dravosburg.

One of the most beautiful bridges that came to mind was the Chesapeake Bay Bridge which she flew over on her routes to Washington. Staying over in that area was always a treat because there were so many restaurants to have dinner and drinks in with old friends, such as Benjamin King and Henry Rough, an executive at the Civil Aeronautics Authority, who lived and worked in Washington, D.C.. Those were some of the many happy memories of her days with Central Airlines where she accomplished what no other female pilot of her time had done by becoming the first to hold that position. But, all good things have a tendency to come to an end at some point in time. Helen just didn't expect it to come about so suddenly.

The more she thought about how unfairly the pilots' union had treated her, the harder she pushed her plane. Not letting her join didn't bother her that much. Who cared? But to say she was unable to pilot a plane during rainy or stormy conditions was like drawing a line in the sand. It was ridiculous! She had been flying for over five years in rain, snow, ice, and wind with no mishaps. Helen admitted that was what made her the pilot she was today. But rather than fight the issue she simply resigned. Central Airlines jumped to admit it was a public relations move to employ a female. However, it back fired when the pilots' union felt that more women might be hired to take future jobs away from them.

Oh, how Amelia came to Helen's aid in the midst of the controversy. The union's attitude was like a slap in the face to all female pilots who had fought so hard to break records in speed, altitude, and distance. Pilots like Louise Thaden, Pancho Barnes, Ruth Elder, Bobbi Trout, and others relied upon sponsorships. They needed companies that provided oil, equipment, and aircraft manufacturers who offered their latest model planes to be tested in races as well as their endorsements. After all, maintaining an aircraft is costly. Even filing applications to participate in races was expensive. The entire matter just didn't set right with Amelia, who took great pride in representing women pilots. It was getting personal.

A few months later at a luncheon in Washington, D.C. Amelia was asked by a group of Hawaiian woman who arranged the erection of a marker on the Oahu plateau (where Amelia had taken off on her first flight across the Pacific) what they should do with the remaining funds from the project? After a few minutes she replied to the group, "A fund should be organized to shatter the barriers that stand in the road of stopping women from attaining their rightful place in the aviation industry. With such a fund perhaps we can help them to move forward. One girl did succeed in landing a job recently as a copilot on one of the mail lines. What happened? Well, the pilot's union refused to take her in, not because of lack of ability (all of her co-workers admitted she was okay as to flying) but because she was a female. The result of this action was that the Depart-ment of Commerce refused to let her fly passengers in bad weather, so the poor girl could not do her part at all and had to resign."

To Amelia's surprise, her comment was published by the Pan-American Press Bureau and later picked up by other reporting agencies world-wide. Even during a stop in Pittsburgh at the beginning of a ten day lecture tour Amelia stated, "Helen Richey, rather than Amelia Earhart is the nation's greatest aviatrix." To Helen that spoke volumes of mutual respect as professionals and friendship.

Amelia didn't just ride off into the sunset. She contacted another friend of hers, Phoebe Omlie, who was now with the Bureau of Air Commerce in Washington, D.C. A new program was being put into place where pilots were divided into regional areas across the United States to mark rooftops of buildings, factories, and barns. The objective was to inform pilots where the next airport was located to land their aircraft. This was a great opportunity for Helen to be able to learn where every airport or airfield was located in the four regions across the vast United States. Not to mention a respectable income which was always welcomed.

In 1936, after a year of air travel while marking up the East Coast, the central states, mountain states, then to the West Coast, Helen decided to settle in the Los Angeles area. Up and down the West Coast was her assignment. Bringing her thoughts back to the present, she saw that the San Francisco Golden Gate Bridge was coming into the focus. It had been a long day flying. Now all she could think about was landing her plane and, if it wasn't too late, hitching a ride up to Farm Bay. If worst came to worst she would just spend the night and start up the next morning.

By now it was getting too dark outside to continue so she deciding to just get a room at a local lodge nearby for the night. Grabbing dinner she returned to her room to collapse into a warm soft bed. Her mind was working on overtime. She remembered Amelia's excitement as she described the Electra to Helen a few days after the President of Purdue University, Edward Elliott, presented the "Flying Laboratory" to Amelia for a birthday gift. Is that what we were to think? That was what the newspapers published. Over and over in her mind Helen realized the air craft was anything but a science project. She had learned this firsthand during their Bendix Race in September of 1936.

Chapter 3

A Nightmare Comes True

Amelia had asked Helen to be her co-pilot in the Bendix Race right after she had taken possession of the Electra in July of 1936. What a birthday present Helen thought when Amelia told her. Because the race was a few months away, Amelia wanted to get a handle on how it flew by taking several test flights from Burbank to Kansas City. She relied on her mechanics Bo McKneely and Paul Mantz to get their opinion of its performance. It was safe enough but thrusting it through a vigorous race would give them even a better idea of the aircraft's capabilities.

Amelia, Paul, and Bo knew that having Helen co-pilot the Electra during the race would prove to be an asset. Helen knew how planes were built from the engine to the tail. Bo was convinced that Helen could rebuild an engine as good as any mechanic at his hanger.

Helen met up with Amelia in New York. Planes had already arrived and were parked at Floyd Bennett Field when the two of them arrived just hours apart. The odds of them winning were in their favor with the two 539 horse-powered engines. Other participates may have had higher horse-powered engines, but they also had larger aircraft . . . with one exception. Good friends Louise Thaden and Blanche Noyes' Beechcraft was running about 420, was far lighter and could give them the advantage. Nevertheless Amelia and Helen were good competitors and determined to give their all.

It didn't help that one mishap after another took place shortly after takeoff. Helen realized the Electra had been designed by the most qualified aviation engineers Purdue could hire. Not to mention several air craft corporations who funded the project. Helen knew the plane turned over to Amelia had to be more than a birthday gift. Just as Amelia was telling Helen about the Amelia Earhart Research Fund which several aviation corporations funded for Purdue to have the Electra designed, one of the bolts holding down the overhead hatch had loosened. The hatch began to lift up and down as air entered the cabin.

Helen yelled out, "I know this plane has to have automatic pilot!"

Amelia turned it on and they waited for it to kick in. Helen hung onto the lid as tightly as she could while the seconds turned into minutes. Finally the autopilot took over, letting Amelia assist with the lid until they could get it tightened down. They laughed as Helen stated she felt as if the wind was going to suck her right out over Missouri.

Next the Electra developed a problem with the fuel lines. One line was sluggish, but that was cleared out when they stopped to refuel in Kansas City. Once back up in the air they both settled in trying to make up lost time in the race. While Amelia cracked open a can of tomato juice, Helen sipped on coffee from her thermos when the conversations got serious.

That was when Amelia brought up the subject of her world flight. Explaining that, yes, the Electra was to carry out scientific experiments in the area of biology, but there was more on the line that just that. Helen could imagine Amelia flying over five continents with an aircraft of this caliber with a few shelves of ferns. There had to be a lot more to the story. By the time they reached the end of the race at the Los Angeles Mines Field, it wasn't the shock of arriving in fifth place but the details of Amelia's world flight that had her numb.

Now all the pieces of information seemed to be coming together. Helen was committed to uncovering every detail that surrounded why Amelia and Fred did not make it back. Something went deadly wrong from the very beginning.

It was July 3rd, a Saturday, when Bobby and Helen finally sat down together. They last congregated with Amelia and Fred back in May. Just before the world flight departure for Florida took place. The course was altered from the one planed in March. Now in May the world flight route was determined to run east to west. It was one of those decisions made without notification, which drove Amelia crazy while in Farm Bay waiting for the Electra to be fixed.

Helen couldn't imagine Fred not knowing about all the changes from plane parts to routes direction when he was the assigned navigator. Was he even in on any of the planning? Could the other two original members of the team—Paul Mantz and Harry Manning—be aware? Is that why they bailed out on the second attempt planed for a June departure from Miami, Florida going east to west? Perhaps it was thought that Amelia had enough rest while the plane was being fixed? Or was it bad karma to attempt the second time from the exact point? There had to be a reason, but who was calling the shots? Helen had her suspicions, but connecting them was a bigger undertaking than she could ever conceive. Little did she realize that Bobby was about to set her in the right direction. Yes, a fifteen year old boy was on the right track.

Bobby could hardly wait to tell Helen of the radio transmissions he had heard all evening, beginning at 9:30 p.m. and continuing throughout the night. He was convinced that it was Amelia. She was trying to make contact with ships that were in the Pacific in route to her. He knew her voice. After all he had sat facing her, talking with her, and eating meals with her for months. Her voice and mannerisms aren't easy to forget. After all she was Amelia Earhart.

As the conversation went on, he mentioned the different frequencies she was jumping to so that the radiomen could follow her. There were problems I could hear, Bobby told Helen. Then Amelia went on to some sort of letter frequency which didn't work either. She kept on trying to get the radiomen to talk with her, but nothing was working. Helen was curious about the kind of radio Bobby had that enabled him to reach transmissions being sent between an airborne plane and a ship from the South Pacific? So she stopped him in mid-sentence to ask how he could possibly receive their communications?

Bobby explained it was a Philco radio with a super heterodyne! It could receive shortwave transmissions hundreds to thousands of miles away. His father had mounted a sixty-foot copper mesh antenna to the side of their home. So perhaps receiving transmissions in the middle of the Pacific wasn't so unrealistic thought Helen. If Bobby was receiving transmissions, she wondered who else would have similar such equipment? Better yet, what would they do with this information?

Helen asked Bobby if he was able to write down any of the statements made by Amelia. Did he have it on paper? He stated he didn't have a pencil or paper in the living room, but using a letter opener he found on the coffee table he was able to scratch her transmissions on the side of the fireplace. Some of the transmissions began to come in after their departure from Lae, New Guinea. Bobby raddled off names such as Harry Balfour, The Big Arch, Turk Island, and Line of Position 157 dash 337, Marshalls Island, the Equator . . . he went on and on.

How could such a boy have gathered this much information? By now she could see Bobby was upset, but she couldn't think of anything to say that would help him understand or relieve his mind of worry. She just let Bobby know that she believed him and would follow up on every lead she could find to get answers to what happened to Amelia and Fred on July 2, 1937. With that said, Bobby appeared to calm down. Driving Bobby home she assured him she would stay in touch.

While returning to her apartment Helen recalled the day Amelia told her what was really on her mind friend-to-friend, while sitting side-by-side in the Electra during the Bendix Race. Her concerns definitely over shadowed the excitement of the world flight in more ways than one.

Chapter 4

The Price Tag

Bright and early the next morning after the race, several pilots gathered to prepare for their return trip home. Louise Thaden and Blanch Noyes were still hounded by reporters and fans. Walking through the crowd, Helen spotted Amelia in the middle of two newsreels recording her conversation with a reporter. As she approached the area of the interview, Amelia was explaining her upcoming flight around the world which would take place in March of 1937. Just six months away with a lot of planning still to be made considering how the plane performed in this race, Helen thought to herself. If the Bendix race and merely flying around the United States is considered testing out the Electra, then Amelia's developers by no means had built a plane that would endure the long-distance flight she and her crew were about to undertake. Anticipated stops wouldn't be just for refueling, but for rebuilding.

Helen was sick to her stomach over this arranged career-toppling business. To her, it was appearing more and more like a conspiracy of some type. She just didn't have enough information yet to determine WHY and

WHO was behind the scenes pulling the strings. Could it be political? Perhaps military, for some reason that kept of coming into play. After all everyone knew the Japanese dominated that side of the ocean from Hawaii down practically to Australia.

Once the interview had concluded, Amelia walked over to Helen with the reporter following closely behind. Helen was introduced to him and his crew as he quickly opened his microphone, motioning to the camera man to begin filming. He asked Helen for her thoughts on the Bendix Race. She made light of the experience, carefully not giving up any of her real concerns. It wasn't the time or place for that to be aired. Thanking the pilots for their time, the reporter went on with his crew to catch up with other fans.

The coffee shop next to the hanger was still serving breakfast so Amelia and Helen walked over to it. Once inside they spotted an empty booth in a quiet section. As soon as they settled in, a waitress approached to take their order. With Helen's light-hearted sense of humor she laughed off the race by saying, "We'll take our marbles home and try again next year!"

With a chuckle Amelia sat back and reached for her purse, "Don't cry over the whole thing, kid!"

"What are you looking for in there, a handkerchief?" asked Helen.

"No," laughed Amelia. "This is what I wanted to show you." She opened her brown-leather wallet and pulled out a small folded piece of paper. Unfolding it carefully, she reached over the table handing it to Helen, who slowly reached for it. "Go ahead read it," Amelia urged.

After a quick look, Helen was puzzled. "This is a bill of sale with Clara Livingston's name on it as the rightful owner of the Electra," she remarked.

Amelia explained it had arrived in an envelope addressed to George. "Why would Clara's name be recorded when she doesn't even reside in the United States," questioned Amelia.

"The last I heard, wasn't she living somewhere near Cuba on a plantation?" asked Helen. "I remember Clara at out Ninety-Nines meetings in the early 1930's at Valley Stream, Long Island."

"Yes, she was a member. But now she has taken over her family grapefruit and coconut business in San Juan, Puerto Rico. What is so interesting, Helen, is that Fred and I are to make our first layover at her home. I'm convinced they are using every person I have ever known in one way or another to their advantage. Regardless, have they no conscience?" added Amelia.

Amelia then informed Helen that she learned the funding for the Electra came from three sources. "First, would you believe from our sponsor of the Bendix Race, Vincent?" As Helen shook her head from side to side, Amelia continued, "Next, is J. K. Lilly, a Purdue alumni member. You must know him. He is one of the wealthiest pharmaceutical owners in the entire world! Now brace yourself, Helen, for the third name on the list." Amelia knew Helen would have never suspected the next name: Floyd Odlem of all people!

"So, are you saying Jackie was in on it, too?" asked Helen.

"What's your guess?" said Amelia.

By now Helen was dazed. "This mystery grows every time we talk," she said. "Like the rest of the public I was under the impression Purdue University funded the Electra for you to transport plant life as an experiment in altitude verses growth. After all, the 'Flying Laboratory' was documented in newspaper articles across the country."

"Look Helen, I'm just getting started with the details I've found out. The best part of the entire Purdue project was that I was to write a book based on my flight. Which would become the sole property of Purdue, and the Electra would be theirs also."

George was also going to write a book. Helen could see Amelia was hurt by the plans everyone had made on her back. It was all a mess. Nothing was what it had been set out to be. She felt like a fool with all the publicity that was swelling. The only way to save face was to go along with the undertaking. So much for retiring from all the limelight which had been following her for a decade. All Amelia ever wanted was to further women's opportunities in the field of aviation. While others—from investors to politicians—had their own private motives. It was a shame that the coming together of means, motive, and opportunity was spelling out a disaster.

It appeared Amelia's fate had already been decided for her. The old saying to be careful of what you wish for was now becoming a reality in more ways than one.

Amelia pointed to a line drawn on the sheet of paper. "See that line with the arrow pointing to Franklin and Eleanor Roosevelt? Well, that was also another assignment. I was to assist with his Democratic State Convention in New York. My job at that event was to appear as a speaker. Now my connection with the political arena is established, and I have no say in these matters. As George would say, we need the exposure. It brings in the funds which keeps us afloat."

Amelia's eyes slowly looked down at the piece of paper. Looking up at Helen she stated, "I'm in over my head."

The only response Helen could give her was that there is always a way out of any situation. They just had to put their heads together to figure out a solution.

"If it was up to me to have someone along for the world flight, I would insist upon you, Helen," said Amelia, "but I was informed by the Naval Office that Captain Harry Manning and a pilot who flew China Clippers by the name of Fred Noonan have been selected to support the flight. Paul Mantz will advise it technically."

"He knows his planes. You'll be in good hands with him," Helen reassured her. "The others I don't know much about. It does have the prospect of a military-type agenda. Which doesn't surprise me," she added under her breath.

Amelia knew Helen would figure it out in due time now that all the pieces to the puzzle were being revealed. In her opinion, this plot had to have been carefully thought out. The eyes of the world would be looking on, so there was no room for errors. But there are instances when errors create just another avenue to explore. Will the end justify the means? Or did the price tag cost them their lives?

Chapter 5

Comparing Notes

The original March schedule was for Amelia and Fred to fly west to east via Oakland to Hawaii on down to Howland. In June it was changed to east to west with Florida becoming the starting point. They would then proceeding on a course down to South America, across the Atlantic Ocean to Africa, up to the Middle East, down to the Far East and straight up the Pacific Ocean to their final destination, Howland Island. The route made no sense to Helen. It was one of those decisions made without notification which drove Amelia crazy while at Farm Bay waiting the rebuilding of parts of the Electra after their first attempt in March.

Helen could not imagine Fred not knowing about all the changes from plane parts to route when HE was the navigator. Was he in the group or an outsider looking in as Amelia was? Why did Capt. Harry Manning and Paul Mantz decide not to go along on Amelia's second attempt? Did the route change become the contributing factor for the two men to bail out? Or were they asked to abort the trip by some higher-ranking personnel? There had to be a reason, Helen thought.

Her mind was spinning from Amelia's flying abilities to pilot the Electra, to all the advanced equipment installed, to the true reason behind the flight in the first place . . . a mission for the government. It added up: strange men coming to the house to see George, bills for plane repairs no longer arriving, signing documents that naval officers presented to her and Fred while at Farm Bay, being sworn in to the United States Air Forces with Major General Oscar Westover as a witness, a visit by one of President Roosevelt's advisers, Bernard Baruch, and so on.

Surely Amelia had to know what was going on by then. But like she admitted, "I'm in over my head." How could she back out on an already highly-publicized world event? The trusted individuals that Amelia confided in couldn't stop this runaway train. Nothing is worse than to stand while fearing what could and eventually does transpire.

How Bobby would deal with a tragedy, if the worse did happen, now became a real concern for Helen. To the young boy, Amelia Earhart was not just another miscellaneous airport pilot., someone that he said hello and goodbye to in passing. In Bobby's world, she became a close friend and spent a lot of time in conversation with him during those three months.

George Putnam, on the other hand, had no use for Bobby. One evening while Bobby was riding his bicycle home from the diner, George drove his car along side of him, yelling out his window for Bobby to stay away from Earhart or else. Leaving behind a cloud of dust and a scared boy, George spun away down the road in his big black sedan. Helen wondered if he did that to safeguard Bobby or did he fear Bobby was getting too close to discovering the details behind the flight.

Did George and others suspect Helen of knowing too much, too? After all, Helen was Amelia's close friend for years. Their friendship dates back to 1929. Other than family, there weren't too many individuals who knew Amelia that long. Pilots, especially the women, shared a bond during that Golden Age of Aviation. In order for people to take them seriously they had to support each other. Amelia never hesitated. She welcomed any opportunity to assist others. Whether it was in front of a classroom at Purdue University or in a hanger at a local airport helping a mechanic, she offered a hand. Now who was offering her a hand up now?

Opening the door of her apartment felt good to Helen. The familiar surroundings brought her a measure of peace as she prepared to crawl into bed. The tensions building while traveling back from Pennsylvania had finally caught up to her—all the excitement of the wedding and the anxiety of the possibility that the Electra could be lost due to weather conditions or the Japanese spotting them and forcing the Electra out of the sky. Helen knew the Japanese had very small planes called Zero's that flew extremely fast. They had guns attached and could fire upon any planes that flew over their mandates scattered throughout the Pacific Ocean.

Convinced that her imagination was working overtime, she puffed up her pillow, pulled the sheets up to her neck, and closed her eyes, hoping that tomorrow would bring some long-awaited good news about their whereabouts. As her eye lids got heavier and heavier, Helen kept reciting these word—means, motive, and opportunity . . . means, motive and opportunity—until she fell asleep.

Chapter 6

Behind The Scenes

A scene from the documentary by author, Andrea Niapas:
Close To Closure, The Mystery of Amelia Earhart. 2007

Opens with a group of men gathered around forming a semi-circle drinking glasses of wine. The men are dressed in suites. There are five men with the sixth older in a wheelchair positioned in the center. The conversation goes like this.......

Commander Rob   Gentlemen
                  Our Naval forces in the South
                  Pacific islands. It is confirmed that
                  Japanese forces are expanding.
                  Indeed, the United States can no
                  longer stand by and ignore it.
                  Gentlemen, I believe I was the first
                  to inform you that Japan in
                  fact has been a threat to us for
                  many years.

Vic   How so?

Commander Rob   They feel our military is weak!
Our policy of isolation and
     morality will be our

downfall.

Colonel Jones   Also, Hitler is building up his army.
Once countries that held a military
    presence in the Pacific are
      abandoning their
installations and   returning to
their countries to   support the
war in Europe.

Commander Rob   While the cats away the mice will
    play. No doubt the Japanese
have   been very busy.

Colonel Jones   Japanese have been building up
installations as far back as 1923.
According to Brigadier General Bill
    Mitchells' 1924 report on
page   94... Here it is in black and
white!

    (Hands folder off to Commander
Rob)

    A clear warning!

Commander Rob   Basically....gentlemen. The
    Japanese Imperial Navy has
been   building up so much in the
past   decade it is truly a
combatant to   be reckoned with.

Mr. President, we fear their force
will be at our countries door
step before we know it!

Dave Bruce My God!
(Opens folder)

They can invade us through
Hawaii or California. We're
sitting ducks!

Neal The country is still rebounding.
from the Depression. We
have bread lines in the streets.
Now we're on the heels of a
Japanese invasion! Our citizens
wouldn't stand for it!

(All together agreeing)

Vic (Stands up)
Gentlemen... Please!
(Men quiet own)

Pres. Roosevelt Gentlemen. You all have brought
to light some very serious
issues.
I concur; we must protect our
shores at all cost! But the
last thing I would want is for the
United States to be
dragged into another war.

Commander Rob

foothold onto
ourselves.

The only way out as I see it, Mr.
President is to get a
one of those atolls

Neal

Phoenix

But how? There are the Mariana's,
the Caroline's, Gilbert's,

Islands and 1,000 others scattered
throughout the Pacific

Ocean!
that

Have we the manpower for
kind of coverage?

Dave

Am. . . I missing something here?
Gentlemen. What about the
Treaty of Versailles?

Colonel Jones

we
is
right

(Col. Jones stands up)
They never honored the Treaty of
Versailles! Right now. . .as
speak. . .the Japanese Army
pushing the Chinese borders
up Russia's ass!

Commander Rob

I wouldn't doubt that for one
minute. The want it all!

(Group all together. . .)

That's right!

Pres. Roosevelt

We all know what the end result
could be. . . . The question is

. . .   how do we prevent it? I'm
open   for suggestions. A plan. . .
              something . . .

Colonel Jones   Mr. President, if I may.

Pres. Roosevelt   Yes, Colonel Jones you have my
                       undivided attention.

Colonel Jones   Commander Rob will agree from a
                       military standpoint that our
past   experiences scouting out
                          territories were
vague. Especially   men when it
came to the islands   in the Pacific.
Why is the
          overwhelming question?

Commander Rob   The answer lies with one
                       overbearing person!
Yamamoto!

                    His Navy watches every vessel
                       military or civilian that sails
                    anywhere near Turk, Saipan, Mito,
                       Howland island to name a
few.

                    He has eyes everywhere!
                    We have learned from the past we
                       cannot go anywhere near
them or   we will suffer the
consequences!

Colonel Jones   That included any flyovers. The
                       only ones ever able to get

within   the regions of any of those
atolls   are the China Clippers.
Because   their route takes
them from   Hawaii to the
tip of South America   were airmail
is dropped. Now,   what we
need gentlemen. . .is a
     aircraft to fly over key positions to
       see exactly what the Japanese
         Army and Navy are up to.
           Commander Rob and I are
certain   that airfields have
been built as   well as gas storage
tanks   mounted.
Strategically located for   refueling along their destination
         routes. And believe me men. . .
          they probably have more
than just   one! Now, if we had
a aircraft   equipped with a
mounted aerial   camera
taking photographs while   flying
over head of their territories   we
would have undeniable proof
     of what is precisely transpiring!

         (Group...all in agreement)

         "That's right....That's right!"

Pres. Roosevelt   The problem is, under the current
         mandates we cannot send
military   personnel out on a

scouting   mission. But.
. .perhaps a civilian?

Neal   Yes. . . .That just might work.
                        But whom can we turn to?

Dave   Someone, no one would ever
                                expect. Yet. . .alone the
Japanese.

Vic   Yes, where is Cedric Smith when
                                you need him? Now he
would   think of such a person.

                        (Pause)

Dave   Now....wait a minute. I read
                        George Putnam announced
in the   New York Times the other
day   that Amelia Earhart is
planning a   round-the-world
flight to top off   her career. I
don't know how far   along they
are in their planning   stage. It
couldn't hurt to give
        George a call.

Neal   More importantly, where are they
                                getting their funding? Plane,
fuel,

                        manpower and so forth. That
                                carries a hefty price tag.

Vic   Why not recruit her? She's already
                          a national hero.

Commander Rob   She'll be able to keep us closely
                          informed of sightings at all
times   as well as taking
photographs of   any activity
while flying over the   atolls. Best of
all we can update   our maps
which gentlemen
          haven't been done since World
                War I.

Vic   And who would ever expect a
                          woman such as Amelia
Earhart?

                       (Everyone laughs together)

                       Certainly....not me!

Dave   Knowing Putnam he'll probably
want

                        write a book on the   entire affair.
                       "Amelia Earhart goes down in
                       history as not only the first woman
                       to cross the Atlantic, but to fly
                       around the world!"

                       (Everyone laughs together)

Pres. Roosevelt   No mistakes...gentlemen! I want
                          nothing to go wrong! Do I

make   myself perfectly clear? The
                                     American people
must know   NOTHING of
this.

Colonel Jones   Earhart is the best woman pilot
                                around. But she'll need a
                                navigator that knows
the Pacific   route. Now. . .Fred
Noonan comes   to mind. His
work for the Office of   Naval
Intelligence as well as his
                          outstanding reputations of Naval
                                navigation and intelligence
career   makes him my choice! I'm
sure   you all would agree?

                    (Several in agreement respond)

                              "Sure"!

Pres. Roosevelt   I'm all in favor.
                                Any objections?

(Group raise their glasses of wine to toast each other as
          conversations among themselves begin)
                Scene closes as it fades out.

March 20, 1937 marks Amelia Earhart, Paul Mantz, Harry
Manning, and Fred Noonan's take off and first world flight
attempt.

Amelia Earhart and Fred Noonan began a second attempt
the end of May 1937.

Chapter 7

White House, Reaction

A scene from the documentary by author, Andrea Niapas: *Close To Closure, The Mystery of Amelia Earhart*. 2007

Scene opens in the map room of the White House.

Note: July 2, 1937   Notification of fliers lost at sea

McGary   All rise!

                          (Enter Pres. Roosevelt)

Pres. Roosevelt   Please be seated men.

     Adm. King   Mr. President. We have just
                                received a urgent wire from
Capt.   Miller of the Itasca stationed
                          at
                          Midway.

Pres. Roosevelt   Please, Harry, continue.

Adm. King   A plane has been shot down near
                        Mili Atoll by the Japanese
Imperial   Navy. At this time it
is uncertain of   any survivors.
The Itasca is in   route
to Mili as we speak. I'm sure   the
British are in route too.

Sec. of State   Earhart and Noonan had to have
                        been seen by the Japanese
ships
                    which sail between the Gilbert
                        Islands from Lae, New
Guinea. It is   all open water.

Gen. Preston   That's where everything went to
                        hell!

Pres. Roosevelt   Dam it! This wasn't opposed to
                        happen! I want answers. . . .
.!
                    I want answers NOW!

Adm. King   Mr. President. The Itasca picked
                        up several of Earhart's
messages   but each were sent
on different   frequencies. She
constantly   jumped on
one line than jumped   to another.
They were so badly   garbled that
the radio men   couldn't
pinpoint her exact
        position. I don't think she had

enough training on radio
transmitting. Jumping from 3105
kHz to KHAQQ then she
stopped   the letter Frequency
and back to   staying on voice. It
was just a   mess for the radio
men to sort out   as they tried
to around the clock.   But to no
avail.

(Gets up from seat walks to map)

Gen. Preston   I bet my pension the Japanese
                          Navy heard every word she
said

                      loud and clear.

(At the map point to her route)

They know exactly where she was
                      headed. Within the first
hundred   miles from takeoff.
As they   maneuvered
North up to the
        Marshall's.

Adm. King   If that's so. . . .
                      She blew the cover of the mission!

Sec. of State   How so?

Adm. King   By broadcasting the names of the
                          islands they were flying

over. She   gave away her
position.

Pres. Roosevelt   Was Noonan on any of the
                                    messages?

Adm. King   No. They didn't pick him up, sir.
                                 I'll bet he convinced her to turn in
                                        a Southeasterly direction for
a
                                 different vector. For that would
                                        have been the logical course
to   take under the
circumstances.

Pres. Roosevelt   Which would have got them out
                                    of a dangerous situation.

Adm. King   It is obvious Earhart was striving
                                    to get back onto the line of
                                        position. . .the
equator. By trying   to keep the
plane lined on the   bearings of
157-337. Which was   her final
radio transmission that   the
Itasca picked up?

Gen Preston   Yes, by then it was too late!

                                (Turns to the map to point to route)

                                Here is the Southeastern position.
                                At Phoenix Island just past
                                        Canton. Wheels up on Hull

Island   is the last part of the radio
                                           message the two
radio men could   make out.

Sec. of State   Which makes that the destination
                                      they were trying to reach?

Adm. King   That's what I think. Of course, the
                                      Itasca orders were for them
to   station ships between the
Gilbert   Islands and Howland
Islands for   any drops.

McGray   She was so close to Howland, too.
                       Dear God what a tragedy.
                                      (Shaking his head)

Sec. of State   We had reports of typhoon
                                           conditions for that area 24
hours   prior to them reaching
Howland.

                       I'm sure that didn't help the last
                                      leg of the flight either.

Gen. Preston   Noonan had flown the Pacific for
                                      years. He was no stranger to
                                      typhoons.

Sec. of State   But was Earhart?

Pres. Roosevelt   Weather, Japanese, British planes
                                      in the area. . . . What else
could   have gone wrong? Get as
many   ships as you can to proceed

in the   direction of the Gilbert and
                                    Marshall Islands.

                        Grace, put a press release out.
                        "Earhart's plane is lost. Air and
                                    Sea search is underway."

Grace   Yes, Mr. President

Pres. Roosevelt   Things are only going to get worst.
                        I should have never gone along
                                    with this plan. I'm sure the
                                    Japanese have both
of them by   now.

Adm. King   Alive. . . .hopefully!

Pres. Roosevelt   Yes. . .but for how long?

(Scene fades out as men continue to talk.
Pres. Roosevelt shakes his head from side to side.)

Awakened by the alarm clock, Helen stared up at the ceiling for a few minutes. Her dream took her back to the day she heard the news. She remembered what her sister Lucille stated to a reporter from the *McKeesport Daily News* when he contacted her for a comment on the disappearance of Amelia Earhart and Fred Noonan.

Her statement ran in the Saturday evening addition of the *Daily News* on July 3, 1937: "Helen will be crushed if Miss Earhart isn't found," Mrs. Lucille Gamble said. "Helen and Amelia are very close friends."

The article further read: Mrs. Gamble said her sister is on the West Coast, where she is engaged in a federal air route marking project. It was through Miss Earhart's influence, according to Mrs. Gamble, that Miss Richey was assigned a western territory in preference to the east.

The Richey and Gamble family members anxiously scanned news reports on the radio as well as newspapers for updates of the search. Each day Helen went to work hopeful of hearing of a rescue. However, by the third week the search parties which focused around the Gilbert Islands were officially instructed to abandon efforts. Ships were directed to return to specified ports.

To Helen's surprise, however, George Putnam, still residing at the Putnam's Hollywood home, was not giving up on the search for Amelia. He kept in contact with the White House, Jackie Cochran and Floyd Odlum. Helen knew of their financial support during the first world flight, which was attempted in Hawaii and resulted in the Electra crashing, damaging the landing gear. Jackie and her husband Floyd picked up a large chuck of the cost to have the plane shipped back to California. What was George up to now she thought?

Helen feared for how Bobby Myers would react to the news of Amelia's death if that turned out to happen. She was feeling ill over it, too. To call Bobby would make things even worse if she had to tell him such bad news over the phone. Sometimes when you don't know what to do, perhaps one shouldn't do anything. The news, of course, was heartbreaking to so many of the pilots she worked with. But nevertheless Helen returned to work to try and keep herself busy.

The weeks and months passed when, from out of the blue, an old friend from McKeesport named Jack Soles who had a real estate business in Beverly Hills contacted her. Jack's family lived a few streets away from the Richey residence back home, and owned several jewelry stores throughout the Mon Valley. Jack and Helen attended high school together. After graduation, like so many others, they went on to college, found jobs, relocated and lost touch. Throughout the next two years they rekindled their friendship and things began to get serious between them.

Since the air marking service was now winding down, it was time for Helen to decide in what direction she wanted her future to go. The subject of marriage had come to the forefront on several occasions. Of course the Richey family back home was delighted to hear the news. However, Helen was having second thoughts. Jack didn't hesitate to present her with an engagement ring she described as being as large as a pear. Helen never wore jewelry to begin with yet alone such a ring. Was she ready to give up her career in exchange for a husband, house, and babies?

While trying to sort out her life, Blanche Noyes, an old pilot friend now residing in Washington, D.C. alerted her to rumors of a war looming in Europe. Even Jackie Cochran confirmed it when Helen and Jack went out to Palm Springs for a few days of fun and sun at Jackie and Floyd's ranch.

No matter how hard Helen tried to justify a change of life style by giving up her lust for adventure, a deep empty pain was felt in her gut. Little did she realize that Jack was planning to ask her to marry him on a trip to Hawaii. But to his surprise (or maybe not) Helen ended the courtship by mid-1939. They remained friends for several years after. We can always speculate about the reasons for her breaking the engagement: she was a free spirit and may not have wanted permanent marital ties, or perhaps she feared embroiling the Soles family in potential harm's way.

It was time to get on with life. Since her apartment lease was running out, it was an omen to return to the East Coast. Within a week Helen was packed up, said her goodbyes to friends she had met while working, and arranged to have dinner with Bobby Myers one last time while in California. Helen knew their paths would cross again because they shared a common thread—their friendship with Amelia Earhart.

Neither would ever forget nor even want to forget that life changing experience. They made a pact to continue to stay in contact, even though Helen knew it would be impossible with war on the horizon. But who's to say they wouldn't years down the road? Life is strange she admitted to Bobby with a wink as they departed in the warm California sunshine.

Chapter 8

Following Headlines

Helen gathered up newspapers that were sent to her from the *Atchison Daily Globe* per a phone call to them before she left California to attend her niece's wedding. She appreciated their kindness in sending them because she wanted to include some material from them in her book. Before folding each paper neatly in half, Helen glanced through the front page stories of all seven of them. She found it disheartening that, after all the accomplishments Amelia had during her spectacular career, the search for her lasted only eighteen days and there were just seven days of newspaper reports.

Helen could only imagine how little she herself would be remembered. Nevertheless she glanced over each bold lettered headline that was wired to news-papers across the United States from Honolulu. They read as follows:

Saturday July 3, 1937   Amelia's Voice Heard by
                                      Amateur Radio

Operator.

Tuesday July 6, 1937	Ships of Three Nations Spur Search for Amelia
Wednesday July 7, 1937	Still No Trace of Lost Fliers
Thursday July 8, 1937	Vast Hunt for Missing Fliers
Friday July 9, 1937	Amelia's Fate Still Mystery
Saturday July 10, 1937	Still No Trace of Lost Fliers Final Stages of Aerial Search This Week-End
Monday July 12, 1937	Little Hope of Finding Fliers

Note: Full front pages can be found in the appendix section of this book.

Chapter 9

Teaching Flight

It had been two years since her last visit to her beloved hometown of McKeesport, Pennsylvania. She couldn't shake the thoughts of a war approaching. Helen was certain Amelia and Fred had to be the first two American casualties of the war which was now simmering in Europe.

Another old friend, Phoebe Omlie, whom Helen worked with in the air marking program, promised to keep in touch with her after the program had phased out. To Helen's surprise Phoebe had taken on another role in the ever-growing need for instructional training of future pilots. Again, the real advancement of a war alerted Helen to yet another area of aviation where she was ready to be involved. She phoned Phoebe, who was now residing in Memphis, Tennessee and told her of her decision. This could be the answer to Helen's dream-come-true job. Combining education and flying were always two important areas of her existence.

Phoebe gave Helen the contact person at the Civil Aeronautics Administration (CAA) who had spearheaded the program. As college administrators around the country heard of the course, action to meet their requests to offer it became imperative. In response the CAA set up tests for pilots who had the prerequisites. If they were interested and passed the test, they would be qualified to teach these courses. Once the call went out for instructors, several technical colleges began to add the instructors to their faculties. The United States military wished to be prepared by having qualified pilots willing and able to enter the Army Air Corp at the drop of a hat when needed.

Helen wasted no time. Within days she had received a packet from the CAA, completed all the necessary paperwork dealing with the course enrollment as an instructor, as well as making arrangements to be relocated to whatever college she was to be assigned.

She talked this career move over with her parents, and Dr. Richey couldn't be happier for his youngest daughter to finally become a teacher. That was the profession he had long hoped to see Helen accept with open arms. Mrs. Richey, in spite of wishing her daughter would settle down and stay in one place, somehow knew that it was never going to happen.

For the next three weeks Helen prepared herself for the test. The test itself was four hours long and consisted of three parts. The first was a flying test, followed by a written test, and then an oral quiz to round out the qualifications needed to complete the exam. Upon completing and passing the CAA examina-tions, each participant would be awarded an instructional ranking to add to their piloting career.

It was no surprise to the Richey family that Helen had passed all three areas of the exam with flying colors. Dr. Richey knew she was a natural-born pilot. She was soon off to New York's Roosevelt field, Matthew-Rappaport, to begin the next chapter of her aviation career. Another first for her: April 1940, CAA Inspector Harry Cullen awarded Helen Richey her instructional ranking, making her the first woman in the state of Pennsylvania to be granted a license to teach.

While awaiting her assignment, Helen took a quick trip back to McKeesport. A meeting of the Aviation Ball committee at the Allegheny County Airport in Pittsburgh, Pennsylvania was scheduled in May. Since Helen was the Chairman of the Women Pilots' Committee, her duty was to contact women pilots to encourage them to attend. In the past Helen was able to urge Ruth Nichols, Louise Thaden, Amelia Earhart, Teresa James, Eleanor Smith, Opal Kunz and many more to fly in for the occasion. The committee was always thrilled to hear who Helen had lined up.

It didn't take long for a letter from the CAA to arrive at the Richey residence addressed to Helen. Waving a small yellow envelope in the air, she announced to her mother that she was now officially notified. Dancing around the living room floor she couldn't wait to share the news with her father. She had only a week to get all her belongs and financial matters in order.

Helen was assigned to the Philadelphia Northeast Airport which was situated very close to the home of her niece, Amy Gamble-Lannan and her husband. Upon calling Amy and telling her about her new job, Amy suggested Helen stay with them. It would not only be a convenient distance to travel back and forth each day, but she would be able to be in the company of family. Amy, however, added one condition. Helen couldn't believe her ears when she heard Amy suggested flying lessons when Helen wanted to pay rent. Nevertheless, it sounded like a win for the both of them.

By June 1, 1940 Helen was teaching flight preparation to her first class of fifteen men. They took notes on every word she spoke as she introduced them to all the instruments and systems of the cockpit.

Part two of the course involved the effects of controls, precision maneuvers, forced landings, stalls and slow flight with an emphases on take-offs and landings. Out of the fifteen students at the beginning of the course by mid-June only ten were still with the program.

By then they were entering into the post-solo maneuvers. Piloting is serious business. Helen needed to instill the critical importance of this third part. She stressed to each student that this is when a pilot must know how to respond to any emergency situation in which he finds himself while maneuvering between the sky and earth.

Cross-country and night flying comprised the last part of their training. Learning how to plan navigations, use the radio, understanding weather conditions, flying across the country, learning landmarks and, of course, night flying. Night flying carries its own dangers as there is a huge difference by comparison to day when a pilot can see land marks. A pilot must know how to read the instruments. His or her life depends upon that ability. So if Helen had to spend a little more time to review that section of the course, she didn't mind at all. She couldn't help but realize that those were some of the handicaps of Amelia's world flight: radio communications and weather conditions. So much depends upon that knowledge and Helen wasn't going to let any of her students fail to understand the functions or every instrument: altimeter, airspeed indicator, oil pressure gage, the oil temperature gage, a tachometer, and compass, to name a few. Then the log book entries. The final part of the course was the written and flight test.

Helen ended her stay in Pennsylvania by the middle of July. Her next transfers moved her up the East Coast to Boston, Massachusetts and then back to the West Coast, Los Angeles Municipal Airport where the Pacific Aero College had twenty-six students enrolled in the program. Helen had to only handle parts one and two because she was needed to instruct at the Graham School of Aviation at the Butler Airport back in Pennsylvania due to a larger than normal enrollment.

With a shortage of instructors, Helen and other instructors were in demand. Keeping busy kept Helen's piloting skills sharp. Practice makes perfect was her motto, and she stressed that to her students. She only wished Amelia had more practice handling the Electra before making the world flight. Pleasing others doesn't necessarily have a happy ending. Perhaps some can walk away while others look over their shoulder for the other shoe to drop. How can they live with themselves? Power is a dangerous vice. Someone or something usually pays the price for the person in power. But who was it in Amelia and Fred's case?

Chapter 10

James's Floral Shop

Once back in Pittsburgh Helen caught up with her old friend Teresa James from Wilkinsburg when she made a brief stop at James's Floral Shop to surprise her mother with a dozen of her favorite yellow roses. They flew in and out of the Wilkinsburg Airport near Graham Boulevard during the early days of their air mail delivery days. Between the both of them, they knew all the routes around Western Pennsylvania like the back of their hands.

That was also the airport Helen flew Amelia in when she was the speaker in a benefit held by the Rotary Club in the Wilkinsburg High School auditorium back in December 9, 1932. Teresa and Helen remembered sitting in the audience listening to details of Amelia's remarkable career and her famous solo flight across the Atlantic Ocean from Newfoundland to Ireland that summer. Questions from students followed. As the lecture came to an end, a reception was held in the green room of the Penn-Lincoln Hotel a few blocks away. After the dinner Helen flew Amelia back to the Putnam residence in Rye, New York from the Wilkinsburg Airport.

Helen was always attending meetings or giving speeches to groups when she was back in town. During a monthly Aero Club meeting at the Allegheny County Airport, Teresa materialized out of the crowd. They couldn't wait to sit down and catch up on what each other had been up to. After the usual casual conver-sation and a few drinks, the discussion turned to serious issues.

Teresa asked Helen if she was aware of the rumor that civilian flying was going to become restricted in the near future. Helen knew of the trouble in Europe and the training of more pilots, but restricting airspace in the United States rendered her speechless. Teresa knew her days of continuing to deliver air mail was also soon coming to an end. Helen asked what she would do if she couldn't fly?

Thinking to herself Teresa stated she would be like a fish out of water. Then she gave Helen something to mull over. "Remember at a 99's meeting a few years ago when Teddy Kenyon suggesting that women could assist in the war effort by ferrying planes? Well, you know I have been checking into that notion. It just so happens that someone near and dear to us both has been busy working out a program women pilots can assist with."

At Helen's blank look, Teresa shouted out, "Think Helen . . . think! Nancy Love!"

Everyone in the room looked over. Helen and Nancy Love both spent a few years in the air marking program which began on the East Coast back in the early 1930's. Teresa up-dated Helen with Nancy's career movers after the program ended. Nancy was residing in Washington, D.C. with her husband, Bob. He had accepted an appointment and commission as a second lieutenant in the Air Corps Reserve. Bob and his old classmate Bill Tunner, a West Point graduate now a captain in the Air

Corps, had been discussing the possibility of Nancy assembling a group of women pilots to be trained to ferry planes.

Teresa explained, "Our job would be picking up damaged planes from air bases that combat pilots flew back to the United States from combat. The ferrying pilots would arrive at the bases and fly those planes to factories to be repaired. We would also transport new planes and repaired planes from the factories to the air bases for the military pilots to return to their missions. We will be saving those pilots precise time. Not to mention we will still be flying and even getting paid too. What do you think about that, Helen?" she asked. "If I receive a letter or telegram from Nancy, I'm signing up immediately with no hesitation. What about you? With all your qualifications, Helen, you would be accepted in a flash."

This really sounds exciting Helen thought. She asked Teresa to pass her name along to the committee in charge of recruiting future women pilots.

By mid-1940, Nancy Love had gotten the opportunity to present her project to Lt. Col Robert Olds. He was very attentive to the advantage of developing such a program of ferrying aircrafts. So he asked Nancy to come up with a list of qualified women pilots who held commercial ratings. Within a week Nancy handed him a list of 105 eligible women.

She even had a name for her program: Women's Air Force Service. However, it took another fifteen months to get the program on paper, trial runs, training courses designed, factories aboard, and air bases participating. All of which had to be prepared before telegrams were sent out to alert the women pilots, who were patiently waiting to serve their country.

On September 6, 1941 the telegrams were sent. Teresa James received hers. By September 15th she reported to New Castle Army Air Base to sign her contract. The first group consisted of twenty-five woman who become known as the "Originals." Helen had heard from Teresa before she reported to New Castle.

Helen was still in McKeesport enrolled in aerobatics training, as well as instructing for the Graham School of Aviation. By the end of summer she had completed 1500 hours at the controls, a milestone only a few female pilots had reached in 1941. Once back in New York, she wanted to rest up and regroup. Her future now held yet another episode which was just about to pick up. However, this particular one would take her over the Atlantic Ocean. But was her best interest in mind as she accepted the position? Only time would tell.

Chapter 11

Two Opposing Views

Once back in New York, Helen thought about writing a book based on her early days of barnstorming, air mailing, flying passengers, and the other women pilots she knew. She contacted her niece Amy Lannan asking her to collect articles the *Daily News* had written about her, photos of the hometown, her old high school yearbook, anything she could get her hands on. Suggest-ing she tuck them away in a trunk for safe keeping, Helen said she would pick them on her next trip home. Amy was excited about the idea and assured her she would get right to it.

Meanwhile, Helen wrote to other friends to send along some of their write ups, too, which she wanted to include. As the weeks went on she was beginning to receive letters from all over the country. One day when she checked her mail box she had received a letter addressed from Palm Springs, California. It could only be from the one person she knew who resided there . . . Jackie Cochran.

She slowly opened the envelope and found it contained a letter informing Helen that Jackie was strongly considering organizing a group of women pilots to travel to England to ferry planes. What was this all about, she thought? Hasn't that venture been already established by Nancy Love according to Teresa some time ago in the U. S. Why would Jackie be interested in perusing the issue? What was she trying to prove by doing so in England?

Helen travelled to Washington, D.C, to see Phoebe Omlie who knew virtually everything that went on in the aviation world since she was involved in the war training of future pilots. Indeed, Helen got an earful of information. It all boiled down to the opposing views between Nancy Love and Jacqueline (Jackie) Cochran as to which one had the strongest pull to get the ferrying program up and running before the other.

Helen was confused because Nancy had the principle concept back in 1940. She had already hand-selected pilots and had them assigned to air bases for training. A name for the program had been established. So what in the world was Jackie trying to accomplish? What was she really up to?

Helen had first met Jackie at a Powder Puff Derby race years earlier and was never impressed with her. Jackie came onto the pilot scene because she wanted to learn to fly a plane so she could get her cosmetic products to stores from coast to coast faster than her competitors. Jackie built Cochran Cosmetics into a successful business in New York. Her products included make-up, hair coloring, and perms. Granted Jackie worked her way up the ladder, but Helen wasn't crazy about her aggressive personality. Helen never quite understood how soft-spoken Amelia coped with it. Jackie had a purpose for just about anything she went after. If not pushing her weight around with her own money, then with her influential husband Floyd Oldum, who was well known in circles of industry, politics and the military. Jackie always got her way.

Helen agreed with others that Jackie was a fair pilot even though she began her career later in life than most of the 99 members of the 1920's and early 1930's. Of course, Jackie had one big advantage over the majority of woman pilots of the Golden Age of Aviation. Jackie had money and power behind her, which was one thing she had in common with Amelia. The only difference was Amelia followed George's marketing ideas. While Floyd Odlum was the big money behind Jackie's ideas.

Odlum was a savvy businessman who dabbled in the area of manufacturing aircraft which was now becoming our country's number-one priority. The Odlums facilitated the finances for the shipment of Amelia's aircraft (back to California) for repairs after her first world flight attempt back in March 1937—which later became known as the "Honolulu fiasco".

There was still suspicion surrounding that mishap, Amelia once confided to Helen. So the connection with Jackie and Floyd was more of an arrangement than what Jackie expressed in public. Helen saw right through her pretense, which is the main reason Helen never trusted her. George, on the other hand, needed the Odlums because they had the kind of money he needed to raise in order to get the plane back to California. The Odlums provided the resources in the blink of an eye. In no time the damaged Electra was aboard the *S.S. Malolo*. Amelia's personal mechanic, Ernie Tissot, was hired to oversee its destination to Oakland, California. Down in aviation history goes Jackie and Floyd Odlum for saving the day.

Helen, however, believed Jackie might be in for the fight of her reputation. Nancy Love got under her skin. So just how was Jackie going to play her hand? Somehow it must have come down to convincing Helen to join the Cochran's team over in England.

This placed Helen in an awkward position since she had already applied to Pan American Airways Africa, Limited, who—with major offensives now erupting in the area—were also seeking pilots to transport French and English troops and supplies to North Africa.

As the weeks passed, Helen weighted all her options. On one hand, the whole idea of flying over Northern Africa was similar to the route Amelia and Fred flew back in June of 1937. There had to be a connection to why their route was designed for them to fly over those particular countries? Now with a possibility of retracing that route Helen wanted to seize the opportunity if offered to her. But to date she hadn't heard a word. Time was running out. Could something have soured her chance to follow this important lead?

The more Helen reviewed Jackie's letter detailing her program, the more inviting it appeared. Of course, once the American girls settled into Commander Pauline Gown's established training program—the British Air Transport Auxiliary—indications were that Jackie planned on returning to the United States. Also revealed in Jackie's letter was the promise of a promotion to Commander of the American pilots. According to Jackie, that would permit Helen the opportunity to have that rank under her belt upon her return to state side. Helen couldn't figure out what she meant by under her belt. If Jackie was offering her anything, surely there was a price to pay. Helen knew no one gets anything for nothing, especially from Jackie Cochran. However, now it appeared she needed a favor. Who else could she leave her command post to? Helen was qualified over and beyond the standards of the other American pilots.

What did Jackie have in mind to do that required her to return to the States weeks after arriving in England? For some reason, Helen knew it had to do with Nancy Love, Jackie's old nemesis. To keep one step ahead of Jackie's game, Helen decided to take her up on the invitation to enlist in the group of pilots going to England. She remembered an old saying that rolled around in her head—keep your friends close but your enemies closer. After all there had to be something in it for Jackie or she wouldn't go after the prize in the first place. Winners don't take to second place too kindly.

Chapter 12

All Aboard!

The requirements to qualify for the volunteer service with the newly formed American woman's section of the British Air Transport Auxiliary began with examinations in the areas of flight testing and physical fitness, all of which were to be done in Montreal, Canada. Jackie also requested a personal interview so each eligible contender scheduled a visit to her Fifth Avenue office in New York City. Helen went right to work completing her application as soon as it arrived.

As she sat tight to hear if she made the cut, Helen put her time to good use by cleaning up her apartment, as well as getting her financial affairs in order. Mean-while Jackie was obligated to pilot a bomber from Montreal over the Atlantic Ocean to England to seal the deal for her personal enterprise. She meant business just as the United States promised Lord Beaverbrook, England's Minister of Military Procurement military supplies. This was her green light to set her program in motion. Of course, General Hap Arnold was her go-to military liaison.

Once in England, Jackie was eager to meet Commander Pauline Gower, head of the English women pilots. She wanted to learn the nuts and bolts of how their program worked. Jackie would use that information as the blueprint in her program. But it took weeks and months of more meetings in Washington D. C. with military officials, President Roosevelt, First Lady Eleanor Roosevelt, and General Hap Arnold to finally obtain the confirmation Jackie needed to place her course in motion. Everything from uniforms and ground school to assigning air bases after graduation had to be completed before the first bus load of women pilots arrived for training at Sweetwater, Texas. She had her hands full setting up her United States' program. First, though, she still had to select the pilots who were to be sent to England. Putting the horse before the cart had to be stressful for Jackie. Meanwhile Nancy Love and her group the "Originals" were already ferrying planes between factories and bases.

With letters and telegrams already circulating throughout the United States, out of a list of 3,000 women pilots Jackie selected forty to interview. By the end of winter 1941, she had eliminated sixteen. A group of twenty-four passed all the requirements needed to make the grade. April 1942 the chosen were ready to journey to England by boat to begin their service.

The first group was transferred over via a PBY Catalina "flying boat". Helen found herself to be among the first group to leave. Also sharing the boat was Virginia Farr, Winnie Rawson Pierce, Louise Schurman, Dorothy Fury, Una Goodwin, Margaret Lennox, Edith Folz-Stearns, Catherine Van Coozer, and Mary Estelle Zerbel. A few days later a ship departed with eight other pilots: Opal Anderson, Suzanne Humphreys-Ford, Virginia Garst, Evelyn Hudson, Nancy Jean Miller, Polly Potter, Grace Stevenson, and Anne Watson-Wood. As luck would have it, a Norwegian Ship called the Mosdale was set to depart

from the harbor with several seats available. So Helen Harrrison, Hazel Raines, Myrtle Allen, Emily Chapin, Roberta Sandoz, and Mary Nicholson were able to jump aboard. They soon caught up with the other eighteen women during a stopover in London, England. There all twenty-four were taken by bus to their final destination: White Waltham Airfield in Maidenhead.

After freshening up and eating lunch, each woman was measured for her uniform. Helen wondered where they were going to be assigned sleeping quarters since the facility was used for ground school? During orientation that question and many others were addressed. Dozens of British homeowners volunteered to house the women, as well as bed-and-breakfasts located near the airfield. There were even accommodations available at the American Red Cross organizations throughout Britain. It appeared to Helen that everything was under control. She could hardly wait to be part of Commander Pauline Gower's Air Transport Auxiliary program which was scheduled to being the next morning. Before adjourning each pilot was given a handbook to review with information outlining the program, requirements, schedules, and so forth, making for some pretty interesting reading that evening as Helen and the others departed until roll call the next morning.

Under a grey cloudy sky the first day of ground school at White Waltham Airfield was in session. Emphasis was placed upon the preparation of handling potential difficulties while airborne, such as problems with the aircraft or weather conditions that can change on a dime between destinations. The focus was to preserve the aircraft at ALL cost. The motto around the pools (flight lines) were, "You are paid to be safe, not brave." Helen memorized Amelia's poem of "Courage," which she would recall during moments of takeoff, as the plane climbed into the sky and the pilot became one with the plane. Leaving all the worries of life on earth behind is for many a relief from the everyday pressures. Upon landing the plane a pilot's mind can be cleared ready to take on incomplete business as well as new ventures. Flying is not for everyone because going up into the unknown takes courage. Helen welcomed every chance to accept the challenge, even during the most critical times of life and death. Flying over unfamiliar land and valleys she went whispering the words Amelia Earhart wrote years ago. . . .

Courage

Courage is the price that life exacts for granting
    peace,
The soul that knows it not, knows no release
From little things;
Knows not the livid loneliness of fear,
Nor mountain heights where bitter joy can hear
The sound of wings.

How can life grant us boon of living, compensate
For dull grey ugliness and pregnant hate
Unless we dare
The soul's dominion? Each time we make a
    choice, we pay
With courage to behold the restless day,
And count it fair.

It didn't take long for the Daily News to contact the Richey family for news of Helen's latest achievement in her career. Janet Kissinger reported that Helen was going to be flying planeloads of bombs from munitions factories to air bases throughout England. According to Dr. Richey and his wife they had received a cablegram from Helen stating she had arrived safely with the other pilots. When asked what he thought of this service, Dr. Richey stated the family was quite used to this sort of thing by now. He explained that Helen had wanted to fly combat aircrafts for a long time and was glad she now had the chance. Behind those words he prayed she would return to tell about her experiences.

Chapter 13

Women's Army Land

As each day came, Helen familiarized herself with British engines and aircrafts, instructions on using Morse code, operations of flare pistol and other signal recognitions and interpretations. A challenge such as flying without radio contact in order not to interfere with the Royal Air Force operations was to some degree difficult to get used to again. It reminded Helen of the days of flying with cloth wings during the Endurance Race over Miami in 1932. Nevertheless she did whatever it took to successfully do her job.

Could this have been the same situation Amelia found herself in while flying toward Howland Island. But why would anyone want to interfere with communications between a pilot and a radioman in Amelia's case? Why couldn't they get onto the same wavelength when there was no other plane in the vicinity? Helen was seeking an understanding to questions that no one seemed to want to address. But she was determined to get further into the mystery surrounding that fatal day. Presently the United States was focused on Germany's efforts to dominate all of Europe, while the Japanese were pushing their way toward the United States by attacking the shorelines of California's coast. The world seemed to be out of sync.

But for now Helen tried to keep focused on the twenty-five navigational flights that were required and the trainee list of destinations. The English countryside looked like a repetitive patchwork of mazes of small fields. It reminded her very much of her days of air marking over the midwest states of Kansas, Illinois, Missouri, and Indiana. The only problem all the women had was the sudden weather changes which were very common in England. If they weren't fighting the rain, the heavy mist at times made it nearly impossible to take off, especially during early mornings. Sunny days were a rarity and welcomed when one would arrive.

By the time Helen reached her twenty-fifth flight she was convinced and confident that she had managed to learn every survival skill known to a pilot, which she considered adding to her planned book of memoirs.

Her next assignment was at a grassy airstrip adjacent to a Spitfire factory in Hamble, Hampshire near Southampton, England called Number 15 Pool. The facility was occupied by twenty women pilots with a number of officers, who managed the map, signals, weather, and transport people. Not to be forgotten, the most important were those who kept the pilots and officers fed, the cook and her helpers.

Another interesting mention Helen wanted to add was the countries other women pilots had arrived from. She had read about these countries in books at school, but never dreamed she would be sharing a classroom with gals from Denmark, Argentina, South Africa, France, Poland, Canada, and Scotland to name a few.

They all were determined to help the war efforts in the only way they knew . . . to fly aircrafts to bases throughout England and France. These gals were pilots who were ready to lay their lives down for world peace. Patriotism runs like red blood through their veins. As confident in their abilities that they were, however, there is always that one crash that a pilots never forgets. No matter how calm, cool, and collected pilots may be, they always remind themselves to expect the unexpected, a piece of advice an old instructor of Helen's expressed early in her career. Helen was no exception to that rule.

It happened one afternoon on a perfectly sunny seventy-four degree summer day in July. Only thirty miles out from Prestwick, Scotland where she was delivering a damaged "Big Fish" Barracuda. As she covered mile after mile, Helen's gut was telling her that the plane wasn't going to make it to the airfield near Chester. Scottish geography is vastly different from England. The route she had to fly brought her up the Perth Valley, north of Glasgow, and was designed to give the pilot an advantage over the hilly terrain. Peering down to the ground, Helen felt the mountain range below was nothing in comparison to those she flew over during 1930's California to New York races.

The sound of the engine of this Barracuda was so rough it sounded as if it was about to come to a grinding stop at any minute. Just then she felt the speed dropping. Lowering the plane she spotted a grassy flat area and began to slowly descend. Switching the landing gear button on and praying the wheels would drop, she closed her eyes. When the sound of spinning wheels was heard, Helen know she could bring the "Big Fish" down in one piece. She wasn't going to crash. So with a wing and a pray Helen brought the beast down in one piece. She hung tightly onto the stick, and there was no way in hell she was going to let go. Once on the ground, the plane rolled hundreds of yards until it finally came to a dead stop with the wheels deeply set into the grassy earth.

Helen was able to unfasten herself from her seat and climb out the side door onto the wing where she could take a deep breath of fresh air. She saw three girls dressed in brown breeches, gum boots, and green pullover sweaters running in her direction. A girl on a farm tractor came from the opposite direction.

Brushing dirt off her uniform Helen carefully walked around the plane to assess damages. Reaching back into the cockpit of the plane, Helen tried using an old radio transmitter to make contact with headquarters to report the mishap. Knowing it was unusual to even have a plane with a radio, she wasn't putting too much hope on it even working, especially considering the age of the plane in the first place. Nevertheless it was worth the try. None of her attempts were successful, so that idea was out.

"Are you okay?" yelled out the girls.

"Yes," yelled back Helen.

The girls were overwhelmed to see an aircraft planted in the middle of a sheep pasture. By now the girl driving the tractor had joined the group. "My name is Jean and there is a telephone in the main house. I'm sure Mrs. Harr will let you use it if you need to. Come on and jump on the side step of the tractor and Margaret will drive you back to the farm house."

As the tractor dodged sheep grazing in the large pasture, the driver made her way back onto the main road leading up to the front of the farm house. When the tractor finally stopped by some steps by the front porch, the land owner and several of his helpers gathered around their visitor. Helen introduced herself as the elderly man extended his hand to welcome her. Just then a lady came out the screen door motioned for Helen to come in the house. She stated her name was Mrs. Harr as she quickly filled a kettle with water and placed it on the stove for tea, while her daughter prepared a bowl of steaming lamb stew for their guest.

Jean informed Mrs. Harr that Helen urgently needed to use the telephone to call her headquarters, and Mr. Harr quickly motioned Helen to the phone. Helen dialed the number, and the call was immediately put through. She was instructed to remain at the farm until personnel from the airfield reached her. Normally a car would be sent with mechanics to see if the plane could be restarted or fixed enough to fly back to the airfield. Knowing it would take hours, if not until the next day depending what the schedules were, for help to reach her, Helen decided to sit back and enjoy the visit.

Soon she was seated at a long wooden table with twelve chairs filled with the three girls, the farmer, his wife, children, and a few more men who tended to the farm. They all attentively listened as Helen told them who she was and why she was in England. They sat and stared at her, amazed to meet a real pilot. Helen herself was interested to learn about the woman who came to her aid. They each introduced themselves and provided the county of England they hailed from. Dorothy was from Yorkshire, Margaret from Lancashire, and Jean from Hertfordshire. They had all joined the Women's Land Army. Like Helen, they wanted to help the war effort.

Margaret explained how Lady Denman, with the support of Queen Mary and Queen Elizabeth, gained control of the Land Army from the Ministry of Agriculture. Lady Denman then created a branch at the Women's Institute to recruit women to be trained to do dairy work, general farm work, poultry care, and horticulture. Teachers, office workers, nannies, cooks, health care workers all enrolled in the program. After all, England was an island which needed supplies and food brought in or else the people would starve. The program Lady Denman developed gave woman training in growing and harvesting crops, working as timber measurers for the Forestry Commission, livestock care, processing meat and so forth.

"The pay is good and we save up to send home to our families," added Dorothy.

Helen told the girls that in the United States citizens were being encouraged to grow victory gardens in their backyards and communities. After all, a war cannot be fought on an empty stomach. Sooner or later the war would be at the front door of the United States so everyone was preparing.

Just then the dogs began to bark and two jeeps drove up to the yard and parked. Everyone moved to the front door where the men stood waiting on the porch. Helen thanked Mr. and Mrs. Harr for their hospitality while Margaret, Dorothy, and Jean made sure they gave their home addresses to Helen so they could exchange letters once she returned stateside.

Waving good bye, Helen jumped into one jeep; the other was equipped with plane maintenance tools and parts. Once back in the office at headquarters, Helen began to write up her report of the mishap. After completing it she could hardly wait to get back to her room to get out of her dirty uniform. A nice hot bath to ease the wear and tire of her muscles after that bumpy landing was all she needed.

The other gals had heard of her mishap and were concerned. As she made her way through the living quarters they asked if she was alright or if she needed to see a doctor. Helen just answered them by saying, "It was just another day at the office."

Helen's leave time was soon approaching. She had been flying for over eight weeks straight. Some down time was welcomed. She made arrangements to hop a ride into London and stay at the American Red Cross Club on Charles Street. She planned to do some shopping and just enjoy the down time.

Before she left, she received a call from an old friend—Ernie Pyle, a journalist whom she had known for years back in her racing days. He was fascinated with aviation, adding articles in numerous publications such as the *Washington Daily Post*, aviation magazines, and books. All the women pilots enjoyed adding comments in his articles. During the 1930's, the public couldn't get enough of the high-flying adventures they spoke about. Of course Amelia Earhart had a lot to do with it as did Charles Lindbergh and his wife Ann Morrow. Boy did Helen welcome the chance to see a familiar face so far from home. She was also told Ernie was bringing along Jimmy Doolittle who happened to be in town, too. The hours couldn't go fast enough until they arrived.

The meeting place was to be in the lobby of the Mount Royal Hotel. When Helen arrived she spotted a couch and two large gold Queen Ann chairs near the fireplace. She walked over and sat down to wait. The lobby walls were covered in cherry wood with several huge crystal chandlers hanging throughout the lobby. Ordering a glass of scotch on the rocks Helen sat back in the soft chair and she began to take a sip of it. The Mount Royal Hotel reminded her of the Penn Lincoln Hotel in Wilkinsburg where she and Teresa James would meet for dinner after flying into Pittsburgh. That was also Amelia's favorite place to meet when she flew into the town on her many lecture tours.

About fifteen minutes later Ernie came strolling into the hotel lobby and spotted Helen. Jimmy was going to be late because the trains were behind schedule, so they sat talking about the good old days. This gave him enough news to write up two articles that were going to appear in the *Washington Daily News* October 15th and 21st of 1942. Helen told him all about her Air Transport Auxiliary days, Jacqueline (Jackie) Cochran organizing the group, delivering about 50 or more Spitfires, and so forth. When Ernie asked Helen what one of her dream assignments would be she stated to go along on a raid over Germany and, of course, meet Hanna Reitsch, who was the foremost Nazi Germany test pilot at the Rechlin airport. Not to mention she could fly gliders over the Alps. But for now Helen was winding down her contract with the ATA's.

Ernie brought up the subject of what her next goals would be when she returned to the United States? Helen expressed her desire to write a book covering her career from day one back in 1929 to the present and everything in between.

"Writing about my flying days with all my friends alone would be a book by itself," she laughed.

Ernie agreed. They were all intertwined through races, flying clubs, sponsors, air fields, instructors, barnstorming and so forth.

Then Helen focused in on the mystery of Amelia and Fred during their world flight. Helen stated she was driven to find out what went wrong. Ernie agreed it would make for a very interesting investigation, but felt it would be like trying to find a needle in a hay stack. Ernie knew Helen might be onto something immense and urged caution. He knew she had been good friends with Amelia over the years. He also knew Helen would hold nothing back. She was going to write it.

"Bottoms up," should be the title laughed Helen holding her empty scotch glass up in the air.

Just then Jimmy Doolittle entered the lobby door. They both leaped to their feet to welcome him. After hugs and handshakes, all three were ready to sit down to a good dinner, drinks, and conversation. Helen wanted to learn about his raid over Tokyo and the islands he flew over to get there. Did he spot any plane parts over the South Pacific Ocean or hear rumors about Earhart and Noonan in Washington? Helen knew he would tell her because she considered him a man of impeccable honor.

Chapter 14

Commander Cochran's Announcement

A few days after returning to active duty in Britain, Commander Cochran called all the girls into the dining hall for a meeting. As they followed one another they couldn't help wondering what was up. When Jackie made her dramatic entrance into the room everyone stood at attention and saluted her as she made her way to the front table.

"'Ladies please be seated."

This was unusual because Jackie hadn't had an open forum since their arrival. Helen knew something had to be of critical importance. Jackie informed her pilots that she was returning to the United States because General Arnold of the Army Air Corps had requested that she organize a women's ferrying group. She even had a name selected: The Women's Air Force Service Pilots. Helen thought to herself . . . that's Jackie for you, always one step ahead.

Jackie's next sentence surprised the hell out of Helen. "I will be turning my leadership duties over to pilot Helen Richey! She will now be addressed as Commander Richey, ladies."

A loud standing ovation suddenly ensued. Could this be happening? Why me, she thought? There had to be a catch. As she stood up smiling at the woman, Jackie motioned for her to come up to the table. She pinned a pair of gold bars to Helen's uniform, then shook her hand and offered a salute. Oh boy, Jackie was going through the motions. All Helen wanted to do was find out what this show was all about.

The dining room staff entered with trays filled with a beautiful selection of hors d'oeuvre: olives, anchovies, canapés, cheddar cheese and several breads. Of course no party would be complete without bottles of wine, and Jackie delivered a heartfelt toast. She covering all her bases, from the first time she met Helen to their days racing across the United States as competitors. After all the hoopla was said and done Helen couldn't wait to get Jackie aside to find out the scope of her new responsibilities.

The opportunity didn't arrive until the next morning after breakfast. Helen was asked to meet with Jackie in her office promptly at 8:30 a.m.. With that in mind she wrote down questions for Jackie that she needed to have addressed. One matter certainly needed to be addressed: the end of Helen's initial eighteen-month contract was coming up. Did she have to remain in England? Her head was spinning as she walked to the headquarters building. Jackie's office was located on the second floor in room 214. A secretary greeted her, then proceeded to knock on Jackie's office door to announce her arrival.

The office was large and nicely furnished: carpeted with an attractive couch, soft comfortable chairs, and coffee tables. It looked like the lobby of the Ritz hotel. Not exactly the style Helen expected to see, judging from the outside of the building. She imagined that Commander

Gower's office was nothing in comparison, but recognized that maintaining a first-class image was part of Jackie's style.

Helen was to be in charge of the twenty-five American pilots who remained in the program even though their contracts would also soon be ending. One good thing that did come out of the ATA program were the number of hours logged by the participants during their enrollment. As a result, many of them would now qualify to be considered for enrollment into Jackie's new ferrying group when they returned to the states. At this time, however, only a handful of the pilots appeared to have a serious interest in enlisting with the newly-named Women's Air Service Pilots (WASP) program that Jackie was now excited to get underway. Helen knew Nancy Love already had the program not only in place but up and running. So what was Jackie's rush?

Once they settled down to talk, Jackie began to outline Helen's position. Every detail was typed out in a pamphlet format with paper clips indicating the areas Helen would be especially expected to follow. Helen flipped through the pages, then looked up at Jackie.

When she inquired about the time she was expected to remain in England, Jackie paused for a few seconds then looked across her desk. "By the end of December we should have our duties here completed. If there are any active contracts they should be de-activated. All those that it effects I hope will consider joining the WASPs."

To Helen that sounded possible, but she know many of the woman were married, had jobs back home, or—judging from overheard conversations—had simply had enough of ferrying planes. Even with all this in mind, she didn't want to discourage Jackie so she went along with her explanations and listened closely to her instructions.

Jackie saw an huge advantage to signing these pilots on because, like herself, they knew the drill as well as having accumulated the requisite air hours during their stint in England. Then Jackie opened the flood gates with the truth of the matter. Getting out of her chair she walked over to the window, glanced out then turned back and walked over to Helen. She credited Nancy Love with being an excellent pilot by anyone's standards, but explained that she and Nancy had far different philoso-phies about the pilot recruitment process.

By now Helen was confused. She knew many of the woman Nancy had recruited and, as a group, they had plenty of experience. What could be bothering Jackie about those women? She didn't wait long before the words flowed out of Jackie's mouth.

"The group Nancy has assembled has 500 hours in the air. That makes them an elite group for sure. Far few women have had the privilege or money to accumulate air hours at that rate," declared Jackie.

There it was. Helen determined that this must have been the crux of the issue from the beginning. Helen knew of Jackie's unfortunate past. She was born into a poor family in Florida, and her parents gave her to another family, hardly better off than themselves, to raise. Jackie told others that she even gave herself her own name by looking through a phone book. She supported herself by learning how to fix hair, developing a clientele of wealthy women before relocating to New York. There she worked for beauty shops on Fifth Avenue until she was able to open one of her own.

Always ambitious, by the time Jackie was in her late twenties or early thirties, she developed a thriving

business called the Jacqueline Cochran Cosmetic Company. The company set up a laboratory in Roselle, New Jersey and rented an office in New York City. Jackie was a self-made success. She learned the ropes and pulled herself up from poverty. Helen admired that.

When Jackie met Floyd Odlum, a wealthy business man, at a Florida dinner party, the idea of marriage wasn't far off. Jackie had to wait for him to divorce his wife, but then Floyd was all hers—with a few exceptions. Floyd had two grown children. Jackie enjoyed money and all that money provided for her, but the rags-to-riches chip on her shoulder revealed itself when Nancy Love came into the picture.

For now Helen just decided to take on her new role as commander and to do her best, just as she always strived to do when taking on any assignment. In five months she would be able to return to the United States with a good flying record and that meant the world to her. As the weeks and months passed rapidly by, Helen wrote to her family informing them of her new position and a possible date for returning to McKeesport for some down time.

Helen was so busy she didn't know if she was coming or going: flying planes back and forth, writing reports, handling payroll, and fielding correspondence from Jackie who was now at the WASP's new headquarters in Sweetwater, Texas. The days flew by and before she knew it, she found herself back on a ship en route to the United States with a few more chapters of her book completed.

Once in the states she caught a flight to Pittsburgh, Pennsylvania. She had actually resigned from her position a little sooner than expected due to concern for the failing health of her mother. As she told a reported from the *McKeesport Daily News*, "Family comes first; careers can catch up."

Helen remained at home appreciating precious time spent with her family and friends. Absorbed with all the news and events that were going on at the time, she managed to look through the boxes of photos and newspaper clippings her niece Amy been gathering. Now Helen had a few more items to add to those boxes: her pins from the ATA's, her hat, keepsakes she collected from places she visited during her stay in London, and letters. There were so many odds and ends that she needed another box. A few log books alone could fill a box. Realizing that each item had a story behind it got her thinking about her book again and she spent hours organizing the boxes according to chapters in her career. When she opened a notebook and wrote out a list of chapter headings, Helen knew she was on her way to compiling her memoir.

Chapter 15

God and Country

Out of the blue Helen received a phone call from Teresa James who was in town on leave from the WAFS. Wanting to get together, they decided to meet at Theo's diner in Forest Hills for coffee. Teresa couldn't wait to tell Helen of the latest update around the base where she was already ferrying planes.

When Helen arrived at the diner, Teresa had a table and coffee was ordered. As Helen sat down in the booth there were a few newspaper articles spread out on the table.

"Look at this Helen," exclaimed Teresa. "Jackie's all bent out of shape over Nancy Love's course already being in operation. Now she's trying to change qualifica-tions and even the organization's name. Who gives her the authority?"

"She's Jackie Cochran. She'll be standing way after we're all said and done," chuckled Helen. "Jackie began working on organizing the course when we stepped foot in England almost two years ago to help with the ATA's. That was why we were recruited to go in the first place for—her to study it with Pauline Gower assistance. Let's face it. Cochran's coming to the party a little too late. Now she wants to speed up the show with the desire to take full jurisdiction."

"Look at this letter," Teresa said as she handed it over to Helen. "Kathy Wilson received it a week ago from Jackie. She is trying to recruit any pilot between the ages of 21 and 34, standing at least 62.5 inches tall, and having 200 hours of flying experience. How's that for qualifications?"

"Pauline Gower and her staff handed us a Ferrying Manuel on the first day of ground school," added Helen. "Look, Jackie probably took a little of Pauline's manual and a few pages of Nancy Love's and developed her own qualifications and course. That's Jackie for you, Teresa . . . always one step ahead." Helen was now very interested is seeing exactly how many of her ATA pilots were going to volunteer to step up to the plate and enroll?

"Well, my understanding is that Jackie's intent is to reach out to pilot recruits with an emotional plea for their help in the war effort."

"God and country! All Americans want to do their part . . . look at us," Helen pointed out. "After all, with such a serious shortage of pilots in our country it would be a disgrace not to come forward. Especially if one does have the ability and credentials to do so. Perhaps I'll receive notification soon," she added.

"After all Jackie would have a heart attack if she heard you joined Nancy Love's WAFS," laughed Teresa. "You know, Helen, you should have joined us all along because you are much admired for your career accomplishment by the women pilot community. There is no other pilot more qualified than you, Helen . . . next to me, of course," she added. As they laughed, they drank another cup of coffee and finished up with a piece of hot apple pie topped by a scoop of French vanilla ice cream.

Helen kept herself busy helping around the house, shopping for groceries, and caring for her mother. One afternoon as she was preparing dinner her father, Dr. Richey came into the kitchen holding a letter addressed to her from Jacqueline Cochran. Helen took a deep breath as Dr. Richey handed her the letter over to her.

The return address was Avenger Field, Sweetwater, Texas. Helen had expected that sooner or later Jackie would reach out to her. She opened the envelope and withdrew the letter with a smile on her face. She was surprised that the letter was a standard one.

"Not expecting a letter, Helen"? asked her father.

"Oh, I was expecting one, but thought it would be a little more personal coming from her. Not one that went out to pilots Jackie had never known before," said Helen. Her disappointment could be felt by Dr. Richey as she slowly folded the letter placing it neatly back into the envelope.

The letter requested that a response be made within a week so that an interview could be arranged. Dr. Richey tried to assure her that the real purpose of the letter is to ask for your help. He knew his daughter would take the proper action. After all, she understood all too well that the United States was calling on her to perform a service. That evening Helen called the phone number listed at the bottom of the letter and set up a date for an interview.

In few days a telegram arrived with the date, time, and location for her interview. By the end of the week Helen found herself in Sweetwater, Texas, having a physical exam at the doctor's office at Avenger Field. She was then escorted into another building for a ten- minute interview with Jackie's secretary, Mrs. Leoti (Deedie)

Deaton, who went over salary and class orien-tations, and handed her yet another pamphlet (to add to her box of memoir material). Walking away after the so-called interview, Helen could see Mrs. Deaton didn't have an aviation background because she didn't question any of her professional qualifications. What could that mean? Perhaps Mrs. Deaton knew who Helen was and realized that Helen knew more about aircrafts than anyone on the base. Later that day she heard that Jackie was hand picking twenty-nine women to form Cochran's first training class at Avenger Field.

Jackie was aware the success of her training program depended upon that first class of pilots. Problems soon surfaced that had to be addressed. A large majority of her recruits were arriving with less than 200 hours of flying, which meant that they only qualified for pilot license as a recreational flier. As far as Helen and others who had been flying for years could see, these new pilots would have to become serious pretty quickly or they would be on the next bus back where they came from.

Helen could see that Jackie might have believed Nancy Love's WASF's to be an elite group of pilots in the sense of having had opportunities handed to them more so than others. But, to amass hours in the air takes years of dedicated practice. Her program consisted of three to four courses of ground school, solo, and a first assignment ferrying a C-47 between Chicago and Romulus. All that required plenty of pilot testing before it could be under-taken. Jackie was trying to set up an organization that could enroll and train hundreds of pilots, hopefully balancing out those who would washout, resign, or leave for whatever reason. And, ideally, those who left would do so before much time and effort and expense was involved in training.

There were only a few pilots such as Hazel Raines, Myrtle Allen, Emily Chapin, and Helen who followed up their ATA service with joining the WASP. Catherine Van Doozer was overage, but due to her background she became an establishment officer. Instead of flying, her duties included enrolling new arrivals, supervising conduct and well-being until graduation, handing the paper work of discharges, schedules, and orders to active duty. Although ATA women entered the WASP at different dates, they kept in touch throughout their service and after the war.

The first class (43-1) graduated April 24, 1943. Thirty pilots enroll with twenty-three graduating. By May 28, 1943 (43-2) there were sixty enrolled with forty-three graduating. Two months later by July 3, 1943, fifty-eight were enrolled and thirty-eight graduated. August 7, 1943 (43-4) had the largest number of enrollments into the training program; one hundred and fifty-one enrolled with one hundred and twelve graduating. Helen arrived September 11, 1943 (43-5) as did one hundred and twenty-seven other women. Eighty-five graduated and another hundred and twenty-two arrived October 9, 1943 (43-6) and eighty-four graduated. As 1943 was coming to an end, the class of 43-7 arrived on November 12, 1943, with one hundred and three trainees while half (59) graduated. The last class of the year was 43-8. Less than one hundred (96) entered with half (48) graduating.

The first class of 1944 was to begin February 11, 1944, and the WASP program continued to see more enrollments. The last class to graduate was 44-10 on December 7, 1944. As one hundred and seventeen pilots entered through the gate of Avenger Field for the 318th Woman's Flying Training Program.

Helen couldn't believe she had to go through the entire training program from start to finish. She was so far advanced. Why would Jackie Cochran expect her to do so? How was she given a command post in England a year earlier, only to be placed in a training program virtually at the same level as an inexperienced pilot who had only accumulated fifty hours of flying in their entire career? It just wasn't adding up to Helen. Why would Jackie let this happen?

To Helen it was a low blow. Humiliating. Was that the point? Perhaps Teresa was right, and she should have joined Nancy Love's group years ago. But then she wouldn't have gotten the opportunity to fly for the ATA's. Somewhere in all of this Helen could justify her own decisions. Was this the same catch-22 Amelia got into when she agreed to accept the Electra from Purdue University? Strings are always attached to everything. Guess the old adage to be careful for what you wish for really is true, she thought. Especially if someone else is in the dominate position of power. Power can become a dangerous vice if it over takes one's rational reasoning.

After six to eight weeks of training, Helen was back in the air doing what she did best . . . flying. With all the ratings, advanced instrument courses, pursuit school, and solos under her belt (all which was a review for her), she received her first assignment: Fairfax Field in Kansas City, Missouri. She transferred BT-15's, B-25's, PT's AT's, pursuits, C-47's, and C-45's to New Castle, Delaware. Once again she teamed up with Teresa James who was on active duty in New Castle.

Helen reported to a large white frame building with black lettering above the door reading BOQ (Base Officers' Quarters) #4. The same number which appeared on a set of keys given to her by the duty officer at head-quarters when she signed in upon arrival. One was for the front door and the other for her room, number 28. Unlocking the door she entered a medium-sized room with a few floor rugs, a twin bed, dresser, a desk, and chair. It appeared basic, but after hours of being belted into a hard uncomfortable vibrating seat inside a plane, lying down flat is welcome and any kind of bed feels like a soft cloud.

Helen always made a habit to call her family back in McKeesport as soon as she arrived at a new base to let them know where she was and to put their minds at peace. Spotting a phone on the desk, she dropped her suitcase, small duffle bag, and purse and grabbed the phone's receive while she sat down on the bed. After getting all the latest details of what was going on with her sisters and their children, she informed Dr. Richey that she had just put his birthday gift in the mail. Mrs. Richey was planning a family party and wished Helen could be home for it. Unfortunately, having just arrived, she didn't have any leave time. Her assignment roster had already been documented at headquarters with no breathing room in it to leave on a forty-eight hour pass.

Wishing her father a very happy birthday Helen promised she would fly up as soon as she was eligible to take and would make reservations for everyone at his favorite restaurant—Taylor's—in East McKeesport for a belated birthday party. He agreed and said he would hold her to that promise on her next visit. After telling each other good night, Helen held onto the receiver as it went silent.

Feeling a little sad after hanging up, she decided to unpack her suitcase to keep her mind off home. Next was unloading the duffle bag. To the dresser she went with an armful of underwear, nylons, shirts, and sweaters. As she was tucking them neatly into drawers, the quiet was broken by a few knocks at the door.

As she opened it, a familiar voice yelled out, "Welcome, Kiddo, heard you were assigned to the same floor." With a bottle of scotch and two glasses Teresa walked over to the bed, sat down and proceeded to opened the bottle. Handing Helen a glass she began to pour out the scotch. Making a toast to long-standing friends, safe flying, and happy days ahead they clanged their glasses together. Women passing by Helen's room stepped in to introduce themselves, and before long they gathered downstairs in the lobby to walk to the officers club for dinner.

Lights were out at 8:00 p.m. because wheels were up at 7:00 a.m.. Sleep was essential to keep senses alert. Stiff black coffee was also a necessity. Helen filled up her thermos and carried it along on the cold morning flights.

The next day while looking over the dining room, she spotted the two pilots she was assigned to assist ferrying planes from New Castle to Newark. Josephine Pltz and Floella McIntyre were standing at a nearby table with a few women with the WAFS finishing up their breakfast. The WAFS were great pilots. Since they were enrolled in Nancy Love's original program, which she had designated as the Woman's Air Force Service in 1940, the 25 pilots involved at that time kept that classification. They were easy to spot in a crowd as each displayed an air of confidence that seemed so different from the WASPs. Helen got along with everyone from all walks of life, but in the back of her mind she held those who paid their flying dues in the highest esteem. Flying was her profession, and she took it very seriously. Her fellow pilots would agree that anyone who flew with Helen had better know their business well. Mistakes cause mishaps. That was a belief Helen lived and flew by. Leaving your life in the hands of someone else could be deadly. Something she learned from Amelia's situation only too well.

Checking in at the base post office one evening she received a letter that had been forwarded to her by Mrs. Richey. Inside the first envelope was another letter sent from Bobby Myers. He informed Helen that he had joined the army. Although his mother had to sign for him, he wanted to do his service to his country in its time of need. Currently stationed at Fort Bragg, North Carolina, he was wondering how she was doing? He wrote of his future plan to use his GI bill to attend cooking school after the war. His dream was to open up a diner or restaurant like the one at Bay Farm.

Helen was so happy to hear from him that she wrote him a note telling him that as soon at the war ended they would get together. She made sure to tell him she was writing a book of all her experiences, especially those from back in the days of the Electra being repaired. She knew Bobby's desire to express his views on that, since he and Helen were two people Amelia confided in during those weeks and months at Farm Bay. Not to mention the radio messages Bobby swore he heard made by Amelia the first week of July 1937. That was scratched onto the fireplace in the living room of his family's home.

Helen had committed herself to writing a book reviewing her career, but now decided to take a bolder step. She decided to outline the developments of the world flight and the individuals involved who were close to the final days.

Bobby Myers remained on her mind for days. One evening when she returned to the BOQ, several of the day's newspapers were laying on a table in the entrance. She picked one up and her surprise found a front-page picture of Brigadier General Haywood S. Hansell and a story describing his raid over the Central Pacific. It was the fall of 1944 and preparation for the attack on Japan was now in motion.

She wondered what the armed forces would find on those islands when the war ended and the fortification process began. Would they find any remnants of the Electra, Amelia, or Fred on those isolated mandates? With hundreds of troops making their way by air and sea, Helen was confident the mystery of their whereabouts would be solved. Or would the military as well as the government hid critical information from the public? For whose better interest? Certainly not the relatives of the Amelia and Noonan.

Chapter 16

Tying Loose Ends On Saipan

Secretary of the Navy James Forrestal spent much of his career during the war by visiting European and Pacific war zones. His objective was to learn as much as he could about the military needs of the Unites States' allies and the Navy. He toured several of the mandated islands throughout the Pacific and by July 1944 finally set foot on the beaches of Saipan. His mission was to see for himself the physical condition of the island, but, as Army Sergeant Thomas E. Devine soon became convinced, it was the undercurrents surrounding the loss of aviator Amelia Earhart and her navigator Capt. Fred Noonan that brought the Secretary of the Navy front and center.

Devine surmised there were possibly other related circumstances that motivated Forrestal to focus in on Saipan. He was looking far beyond World War II to post-war Japanese-American relations. If by any chance Amelia Earhart or the Electra was unearthed on the island, that reality could block any international post-war relations. Forrestal, therefore, was very interested in Aslito Field which housed several hangers containing deserted aircraft. Could the Electra be one of them? Sergeant

Thomas Devine knew other military personnel on the island were told to be aware (on the lookout) if they should discover or hear any information from the natives about a white woman and a man landing a plane on the island years ago. All information on that subject matter was considered sensitive and should be reported immediately to their commanding officer.

With that request, Devine knew the cat was out of the bag. He was convinced that the disappearance of Earhart and Noonan might have seemed far removed from any wartime outrage, but the event itself was apparently intimately tied to World War II and its aftermath. If that was the case, then both Earhart and Noonan were the first two casualties of World War II.

Devine's tour was coming to an end. With time to scout around the island he and a group of soldiers stumbled upon a Chamorro cemetery, which was located on the outskirts of Garapan, the one-time administrative capital under the Japanese. They approached the area and spotted a sheet metal building near a temporary gravesite where a native woman dressed in a hospital-type kimono was hanging up clothing to dry in the sun. As they passed, she noticed the insignia on Devine's sleeve. She waved them over and one of the Japanese-American soldier translated what she wanted to tell them. He understood her language, which was identified as Okinawan. Her story is as follows:

Before the invasion she had lived in the area with her husband, a fisherman who was in an off-shore boat. He and his brothers were authorized to bring fish for the people in the internment camp at Camp Susupe. She had followed her husband from the camp, and she and another woman had arranged to wash their clothing while the men were fishing. While washing their clothes they saw a white woman and man. The Okinawan woman tried to demonstrate that the white woman's hair was short by using her hands to pull up her long black hair. Then with her other hand held rigidly flat, she began to firmly chop at her neck. Was she trying to tell them that the woman was being decapitated or just that she had short hair, which was very rarely seen by the natives of Saipan.

Devine was curious and had the interpreter ask the lady if she knew how the white woman and man arrived at the island. She pointed to the sky, then the sea. Falling to her knees, she pointed to the ground. The translator explained that she was telling them they were buried there. Devine noticed no marker, just wild grass from the sandy terrain. The lady stated that the Japanese had killed them and a few other men at the time! By now the sun was setting, so they decided to head back to the base. If only Private Heywood Hunter had brought his camera they could have taken a photo of the site. However, Hunter assured Devine he would return. He came back the next day and took pictures of the grave site and the Okinawan woman.

A few days later a soldier told Devine that a group of military police were digging up a cemetery. No personnel were allowed to get near the site. He later learned the location of the digging was near a cemetery in central Garapan close to a former jail the Japanese had utilized. In later years Devine got in touch with one member of that group of solders, Private 1st Class August Knockemus of Berkeley, Illinois, who corroborated the story.

Which brings us back to the Electra. What happened to Earhart's plane? A few days before completing his tour of duty on Saipan, Devine was at his station sorting out mail for the soldiers when he peered out the window toward the area where several hangers were located.

Military police guarded one of the hangers around the clock which made it a mystery and the subject of much speculation. It was a usual hot steamy 102 degrees in the shade when the smell of gasoline came from the direction of that particular hanger. Before he knew it, the hanger was ablaze. Being mainly constructed of wood, the hanger was engulfed by flames in a matter of minutes. The other hangers were perfectly intact. Why that one? Again, Devine had his suspicions. The icing on the cake came when he spotted a man in a white shirt. He looked far too familiar. Perhaps that was why he came to Saipan in the first place, Devine thought. Whatever, the reason he had been steadfast in seeking out the truth.

By mid-August 1945 it was time for Devine to return to the United States. His discharge papers had finally arrived on August 12th directing him to report to the replacement depot. Soldiers were lining up with their barracks bags yelling out to one another: "Home Alive in '45!" The excitement was a very welcome relief after months of just trying to stay safe to get home!

Officer Liebig was to drive Devine to the replacement depot that afternoon. Just as he and Officer Liedbig came through the door, a young man wearing a t-shirt and dungarees approached them and asked where he could find Devine. When Devine answered the man, he stated he was to follow him. Liebig said his goodbye and shook hands with Devine as the young man directed him to a door leading out the back of the building where a truck was parked. All along Devine was wondering if this was a navy man. The man never gave his name just directions. "Get in, I'm driving you to Tanapag Harbor where a PB2Y seaplane is awaiting to escort you to Honolulu."

Devine stated he didn't want to go to Honolulu and requested to see his orders. The man informed him his orders were to have Thomas Devine flown to Honolulu for a briefing. All that Devine could say was he wanted to get back to the depot! "You can't go back, Devine!" he yelled. "Please! They are waiting for you." By now the young man was getting irritated. Then the real reason for the change of plans was blurted out, "You know about Amelia Earhart!"

He drove the truck faster and it soon reached its destination, a dock at Tanapag Harbor where an officer in uniform was waiting. Told to get out and leave his bags, Devine protested. In his mind, it was all a set-up. There was no way he was boarding that seaplane. The officer was motioning him to come forward and Devine heard the truck gears crank up as it picked up speed and headed back down the dirt road.

Thinking quickly Devine picked up the bag he left on the road, turned and began running in the opposite direction towards another dirt road that eventually intersected the main one. The officer on the dock didn't try to run after him but simply got back into the seaplane, started up the engine and skimmed the water until he had enough speed, then lifted off into the sky.

After walking about half a mile, Devine flagged down a car driving in his direction. When it stopped for him, he threw his bags in the back seat as they drove in the direction of the base. Once back he was immediately asked where he had disappeared to. "Here are your orders you're going by boat . . . pronto! There are five soldiers you're in charge of, too. Good luck, everyone!" Down to the ship he went with his orders in hand.

Thomas Devine's story will be revisited in Chapter 20.

Chapter 17

As The War Draws To A Close

The war was winding down. More and more combat pilots and soldiers were returning to the states each day. By the summer of 1945, as ferrying assignments were slowing down, Helen had been repositioned to New Castle. This left her more time to contemplate organizing ideas and develop her book. She had been waiting for Ernie Pyle's book, *Brave Men,* to arrive. Over a year ago she had received a letter from him alerting her to watch out for its delivery. With all the transferring she had done by the end of 1944, it was no wonder his book never caught up to her.

Ernie did manage to give her his first book, *Here Is Your War,* in 1943 when she visited him and his wife Jerry at their Albuquerque, New Mexico home. Helen was a good friend to them as far back as the 1930's. Ernie's home was always a destination point along the cross-country race circuit. Many of the pilots would stop in to visit, and Ernie would interview them for articles in various newspapers and magazines handling the latest aviation news and events. He shared a drive for adventure with those pilots, which he admitted motivated him to give up his desk job.

As the war in Europe heated up Ernie sought to support our GIs by traveling from base to base throughout England, France, North Africa, and the South Pacific to hear their heartfelt stories. He soon became one of the most famous war correspondents and the soldiers' comrade-in-arms. Living his life on the edge unfortunately came to an end one morning at 10:15 on Le Island, just West of Okinawa. On August 18, 1945 while being driven to Nahu Air Base, Ernie and the soldier driving the jeep were ambushed by a Japanese sniper. Both were shot to death.

Printed in large black lettering on the front page of the *New York Times*, the main headline read: Ernie Pyle Killed In Action. That evening on her way to the dinner Helen picked a newspaper up from a table, tucked it under her arm and grabbed a tray to load up with plates of food. Once she sat down and began eating, she unfolded the paper. Her eyes widened as she focused directly on the headline. Her fork dropped onto the plate with a clang as she clutched the paper with both hands. In shock, she immediately got up from the table and quickly ran to a nearby phone booth just outside the doors in the hallway of the dining hall. Dropping nickels and dimes into the coin slots at the direction of the operator, Helen dialed Jerry Pyle's residence to express her deepest sympathy and to help in any way she could.

During the next three to four months while the days of war were drawing to an end, many of her friends were thinking of what they would be doing once their service was no longer needed. Those that were married were returning to their homes to raise their young children or to start families. Those who were single returned to their jobs or looked for new ones. Even a commission in the Army Air Corp was offered to the women. They could enter with the rank of first lieutenants.

Helen knew exactly what her plans were. She had been compiling chapters for months. Now the time had come for her to script her story. Not too many of her friends knew of her project other than Bobby Myers and her niece Amy Lannan, which is exactly the way Helen wanted things. The fewer people who were aware of the book, the better it was. After all she understood the truth of Amelia's disappearance was going to provoke plenty of people in very high places. That was the risk. Look what happened when Amelia and Fred played their game. Now, in 1945, exactly eight years later, the only one still questioning the fate of the lost pilots was Amelia's mother. Even the woman Fred had married a few weeks prior to that final flight, had now remarried.

Helen was curious to know George's views at this point in time. Was he presently doing anything to investigate what happened? Especially now that the South Pacific was becoming accessible? Helen wondered who would be the first to venture over to look for possible evidence. Only time would tell. All she could do was wait and watch.

World War II ended mid-December 1945. Families were now going to be reunited while less fortunate ones planned funerals. It was a bitter-sweet time for Americans. The GI Bill was issued to those who had served their country to use to further their education or start up businesses, all in the effort to jump start the American economy. Since the WASP were not considered as having military status, they didn't receive anything other than their monthly salary while assisting their counter-parts (combat pilots) during the war. As Florence Shutsy-

Reynolds (44-5) stated, "We were told the war was over. Thank you for your service." They weren't even given bus fare home. Nevertheless the woman made the best of it.

A farewell celebration dinner was arranged at Avenger Field (318th WFTD). All those who were stationed there attended. One of the women christened it "The Last Supper". A photograph was taken as fifty women gathered in fellowship at long tables to reminiscence, laugh, cry, and to break bread for the last time together.

Helen was thankful to have been able to fly down to Sweetwater and participate. But before she packed up her gear to leave, the women of the 2nd FG, New Castle division, posed for a group photo. Among the small unit was Betty Gillis, Nancy Love, Teresa James, Helen, Avanell Pinkley, Helen Mary Clark, Celia Hunter, and Mrs. 'Andy' Anderson, the housekeeper. Helen and Avanell were both based out of the 33rd Ferrying Group at Fairfax Field, Kansas City, Kansas, then transferred to New Castle Army Air Base in Wilmington, Delaware together. All in all they were a close-knit group with hopes to continue their friendships even though they all were dispersing to different parts of the country.

Since Teresa's husband had been killed while serving in Italy, she decided to re-enlist in the Air Force Reserves. Others returned to raise their families as well as continue to fly for fun. While Helen decided to return to McKeesport to visit family and gather up more of her childhood photos and a few of her engagement party photos taken in Hawaii with Jack Soles and his family. She wondered if she had left the engagement ring in her jewelry box or in the Richey family safety deposit box at the bank.

During those quiet moments back in McKeesport, whenever she would walk or drive past the Soles family home, Helen speculated about what might have been if she had accepted Jack's marriage proposal? Perhaps she would have had a home and be raising their children by now. She would have never have had the opportunity to serve her country as a pilot instructor, fly for the British ATA's, or enroll in the WASP program. She would have effectively been grounded, perhaps for life. That price was too dear for such a free-spirited personality like Helen's to pay. Clearing the fog from her mind, she set out to take care of some immediate business.

Leaving McKeesport, she now began carving out yet another road to travel. Being on her own was nothing new to Helen who marched to a different drummer her entire life. With, of course, her parent's input from time to time. A fresh start was what she yearned for. New York City was where the Long Island Flying Club resided. It was one of the largest and most popular pilot gathering locations on the East Coast. Helen felt right at home. Now all she had to do was to get her living arrangements in order so she could finally layout her book. There were plenty of publishing houses she could approach to edit her manuscript. Helen felt there was nothing stopping her from finishing her book now. She just had to be careful.

Chapter 18

Pen To Paper

When Helen was notified by an old WASP friend, Avanell Pinckley, that her cousin was moving out of a Manhattan apartment, Helen jumped at the opportunity to lease it. She couldn't wire the money fast enough. As an added bonus, the apartment was close to where the Long Island Nintey-Nine's flying group had their monthly meetings. She, Amelia, Louise Thaden, and Blanch Noyes were members of that group since it originated in 1929. Amelia had been elected as the first president of the Ninty-Nine's. The name itself had origi-nated from the number of attendees of that very first meeting.

Early in January 1946 restrictions were lifted by the FAA, granting those holding pilots licenses as well as those seeking to obtain permits permission to do so. That kept Helen busy giving lessons and enabled her to earn a guaranteed income. After all, it was an honor and privilege to have the nation's first female commercial pilot share the cockpit with you. Helen was the most sought-after instructor at the East Hampton, Long Island airfield.

Two old acquaintances, Jane Krafton and Betty Ann Dollion of the Chicago Flying Club, showed up during the February Ninety-Nines' meeting. Helen couldn't wait to find out what was going on in Chicago.

After hearing so many complaints about how slow train transportation was from the outskirts of Chicago, they had decided to form a charter company called "The Coupon Clipper Fleet". Jane and Betty Ann flew customers onto a harbor dock, dropping off their passengers in the morning, then flying them back in the evening so they could easily return home.

It sounded like a dream-come-true job to Helen. She believed there had to be a similar charter company operating in New York City because not everyone who worked in the city lived there. New Jersey, Connecticut, Philadelphia, and upstate New York were just a few of the areas with larger populations. The charter business was her first job using the plane her father had purchased for her back in 1931. To Helen those were her happiest days. So why not do it again? Grabbing the telephone book from a nearby desk she thumbed through it until she spotted Downtown Sky Port. Jotting down the phone number she decided to give them a call. After a brief conversation Helen was invited to come down to their Manhattan dock the next morning. The last sentence uttered from the owner was, "Be prepared to fly in your first group of commuters from Sands Point, Long Island. Miss Helen Richey, I'll be counting on you."

Sure enough, Helen was back in the sky doing what she does best—flying. Even with her busy schedule she always found time to continue writing her book. There was a chapter she held open for Bobby Myers. He could add so much based on his friendship with Amelia Earhart and Fred Noonan, and George Putnam telling Bobby to keep whatever information he might have about the World Flight to himself. The black car that nearly ran Bobby over troubled Helen because she knew as much, if not more, about Amelia's situation than anyone. Could she too have been watched in the past? Or was she being watched now? If the truth behind the World Flight and the radio transmission mix-ups should come to light, the American people would demanded answers! Who could afford that to happen? The Earhart and Noonan families had never received any satisfactory conclusion to their mysterious disappearance. What a shame she reflected. Perhaps her book will provide certain insights and the public could to draw their own conclusions. For those that might have profited by the tragedy, well, Helen suspected they could live with their guilt.

Bobby sent her letter indicating he would be visiting New York the end of February and hoping he could meet up with her to go over his notes. She was eager to see him again and quickly answered his letter. He was just a teenager when she last set eyes on him in 1939. With all the pieces of the book coming together Helen had to seriously consider seeking out a publisher. She wished Ernie Pyle was alive to advise her how to go about this. She had some journalistic contacts, but wasn't sure they would take on a book of this nature. Back to the phone book she went to take her chances.

After a few calls she finally reached one that was interested or at least up for the challenge. Redmond Publishing Company was a little publishing house operated by Jo Ann Redmond and her father. They arranged to meet later that week to go over details. Jo Ann recommended a restaurant on Park Avenue that her family owned. It was an out-of-the-way, quiet, and peaceful place with good food to discuss the project.

At the meeting Jo Ann was very interested in the theme and reviewed several of the chapters Helen had already written. Helen explained she had yet to add a chapter from a friend who she would meet with later that month. With all the particulars, such as number of pages, cover design, photos, editing, and cost discussed, Jo Ann presented Helen with a contract. Thrilled to finally see the light at the end of the tunnel, Helen felt she owed that much to her friends, Amelia and Fred.

Bobby Myers arrived at Helen's apartment with his wife to spend a few days visiting all the sights of New York City. During dinner that evening they went over his chapter. He handed her a copy which she assured him she would deliver to her publisher.

Bobby explained he still looks over his shoulder never able, even after all these years, to get the face of George Putnam on that fearful night out of his mind. What could have made Putnam almost ran him off the road as he was bicycling home from the airport? Meeting with Amelia and Fred before their departure to the East Coast to begin their World Flight must have really brought out the worst in him. He hoped Amelia had never seen that side of George. Or, maybe she had and perhaps that may have been one of the reasons why she simply went with the program that was set up for her. Bobby's final words to Helen were to be careful.

Helen cheerfully assured him that she would. With a warm smile she promised that she would keep in touch with him and joked of her plan to eventually deliver a box of books "hot off the press" to him in California.

Helen spent the rest of the summer completing the book. By September Jo Ann was scheduled to take possession of the second re-write. Excited to finally arrive at this point Helen could hardly wait for the door of the restaurant to swing open. Seeing her coming up the sidewalk, Helen sat back on her chair and took a deep breath. While they talked and ate, Jo Ann read numerous pages of the book. Turning to Helen, Jo Ann mentioned her surprise that the manuscript was untitled. She asked Helen if she had any in mind. After pondering for several weeks she had decided on one she liked, but was worried it wasn't good enough. Jo Ann asked to hear it as Helen uttered softly, "Rich in Courage—Silent in Sorrow."

Jo Ann loved the title because it summarized the essence of the theme of Helen's book. Helen felt comfortable with Jo Ann's opinion and an agreement on the title was reached. One more meeting was needed to see the final proof—when Helen would actually see the final version of the book before it went to press—just to review it one last time and verify that everything was correct. Jo Ann penciled in the date of January 2, 1947 in her notebook. Shaking hands, they prepared to exit the restaurant and Jo Ann placed the book in her handbag.

They said their goodbyes and each went in opposite directions. Helen was on her way to the shoe repair shop a few shops down the street when she felt as if someone was following her. As she turned to look behind her, she saw a middle age man in a black suit stop in his tracks and lean up against the building to light his cigarette. She felt a cold chill but just shock it off continuing to walk a few more yards to the shoe repair shop. She quickly darted into the shop and pick up a pair of shoes that needed resoled.

Upon returning to her apartment that afternoon she discovered that the door was unlocked. Confused, she swore she had locked it earlier. Perhaps the landlord had to go in to fix something in the apartment during her absence. Maybe he mistakenly thought he had locked it up or was going to return. Once entering the room, she looked around, but nothing appeared to be disturbed. There was no sign that anyone had been in the apartment, so Helen went ahead and prepared for bed. The next day was Friday which was always one of the most hectic days of the week, beginning from early morning right through till nightfall. While most commuters were trying to get home in the suburbs for the weekend, others were trying to get into the city.

At the insistence of her sister, Helen was planning to return to McKeesport for Christmas. They were excited to hear about her new job, how her book was coming along, and who she was dating. With a suitcase filled with gifts, a rough copy of her book, and some clothes, Helen was ready for a non-stop flight back to Pittsburgh first thing Saturday morning. Leaving New York's concrete city jungle for a quick vacation back home was surely welcomed, even if it was just for a week. The holidays went by too quickly and before she knew it, she was back in her apartment getting ready to make her final appointment with Jo Ann Monday.

It was a sunny warm January day with above normal temperatures melting the snow from the sidewalks. Jo Ann was waiting at the restaurant and waved her over to the table by holding up a copy of *Rich in Courage— Silent in Sorrow* in her right hand. Helen just about jumped over a waitress in her hurry to get to the table. Smiling she held the book in her hands. She couldn't take her eyes off of the book as she marveled over the beautifully designed cover, showing the Electra flying over a body of water with an island beneath it. On the back was a descriptive summary of the author. Helen thought it was beautiful. She flipped through the pages until she reached the photos and glanced through them. Next she browsed each page of Bobby's chapter. Everything was perfect. Helen couldn't be happier. Jo Ann indicated that Helen's order would go to press that week if everything was okay with the sample. Helen agreed it was excellent. Everything she ever imagined it would be. With that in mind, Helen initialed the inside page for Jo Ann as requested, then handed it back to her.

With everything completed Jo Ann opened her purse and placed the book inside for safe keeping. She informed Helen that she would have the presses begin immediately upon her return to the office. Knowing Helen's book would be a popular item, Jo Ann suggested she would press approximately five hundred copies for immediate distribution. It all sounded reasonable to Helen. After all she was new to the entire idea of book publishing and was trusting in Jo Ann's knowledge from start to finish.

When Jo Ann discovered that Helen had no marketing plans in mind to publicize her book, she explained that her publishing house had a marketing campaign manager who could take on the assignment. Assuring Helen that the publicity promotion would lead up to a book signing date which would be arranged within the next few weeks. Helen reached for the bill from their coffee and dessert as Jo Ann said goodbye making her way to the door of the restaurant. With her wallet in hand, Helen walked over to the cashier at the counter to pay.

Just as Helen exited the restaurant she spotted that same man from several weeks ago hanging around the restaurant wearing a black suit, white shirt, and tie. Then out of nowhere, the loud piercing sound of rubber on the pavement stopped her in her tracks. Helen heard people screaming for help up the street from where she was standing. Traffic came to a screeching halt. "Help . . . we need help! A woman was hit by a car! Help . . . over here!"

Helen ran to assist as more people gathered. Police sirens could be heard by now. Upon arriving at the scene Helen couldn't believe her eyes. It was Jo Ann! She could tell by her blue coat. As tears ran down her face, Helen asked the person standing near her if they saw what happened. An older grey-haired woman turned to Helen saying that she watched as a shiny black car came speeding directly toward the lady in the blue coat. She pointed in the direction the car came from. She had no idea why the car was speeding, because there was a stop sign at the curb. Just as the lady stepped off of the curb and put her foot into the street the car hit her straight on. Boom!

Helen noticed Jo Ann's purse was not on the street. Perhaps it was under her body. By now the police had arrived to examine the victim. An officer was looking around on the street. Then the older woman turned back to Helen stating, "If they are trying to find her purse they never will."

"Why," asked Helen.

"Because I saw one of the men from the black car jump out and pick up the purse which was lying next to the lady."

Helen quickly concluded that someone didn't want her book to be published. The questions Helen raised in the book, leading up to the strange disappearance of Earhart and Noonan, now appeared to necessitate the need to tighten the lid of secrecy surrounding the whole matter. The real question was who was at the controls?

Still numb, Helen managed to make her way back to her apartment building, all the while hoping to run into one of the men in a black suit. Boy, would she let him have it. Maybe it would be better if she didn't. Once inside her building, she unlocked her mail box, reached inside to pull out some envelopes, then closed the small door tightly.

Once inside her apartment she locked the door and dropped her coat and the envelopes on the coffee table. She was so upset she didn't know what to do first . . . scream or cry. Dropping to the couch she cried and cried until she couldn't cry any more. Wiping her eyes she picked herself up thinking a cup of hot tea would help. She filled the tea pot with water and set it on the stove to heat up while she got into her pajamas. When the tea pot whistled, she took it off the stove and set an English Breakfast tea bag into the cup. Noticing there were tiny soft white crystals on the table around the sugar bowl, she assumed that she was not careful when last using the sugar. She dipped her teaspoon into the bowl and added two heaping spoonfuls into her tea. Making her way into the bedroom with the evening newspaper in her other hand, she slipped into the bed. By now Helen's head was pounding. The stress and tension had caught up to her. Reaching over to the nearby nightstand where a bottle of aspirin sat, she twisted off the cap and poured two aspirins out onto the palm of her hand. With a quick sip of tea both aspirins were swallowed. Pulling the sheet and blanket up to her waist, she plumped the pillows up behind her back so she could comfortably read the newspaper. All in the attempt to calm her nerves down.

Thinking about Jo Ann, she turned on the television in her room to see if there was any news reported about the hit-and-run that afternoon. She caught the tail end of the broadcast which didn't make any mention of the accident. The morning newspaper definitely would have the report by then. It was now too late to call the office and Helen

didn't have Jo Ann's family phone number, so she just
closed her eyes and said a prayer.

Remembering she needed to call her friend Mary
Parker about a forthcoming Ninety-Nines' meeting she
reached for the phone next to her bed. During their conversation the hit-and-run on Park Avenue was mentioned
because Mary had heard about it on the ten o'clock news.
Helen stated she knew the person who was killed and told
Mary how she knew her. Mary expressed a real concern
for Helen's safety, insisting she would come over to stay
with Helen. No, Helen stated she was alright, just a little
sleepy. Mary told her to make sure her apartment door
was locked and that she would be over first thing in the
morning. Helen told Mary she was fine and took one last
sip of tea as they said good night. Hanging up the phone
Helen felt chilled. Pulling the blanket up to her neck the
room became dark.

Early the next morning Mary phoned Helen. Her
phone rang and rang. Five minutes later, thinking Helen
may be taking a bath, she redialed Helen's phone number.
Again it rang and rang. Now Mary was worried. Making
her way over to the apartment by taxi she climbed up the
steps to the apartment. Pounding on the door over and
over again. Other apartment tenants opened their doors
to see what all the commotion was about. Yelling out to
them that her friend was in there and she was very
concerned for her safety, she requested that someone to
call the landlord to open her apartment door.

Within a few minutes the landlord, Mr. Wright,
appeared carrying a set of keys. "Here it is," he stated as
he put the key into the lock, twisting the doorknob as he
pushed it open. Helen was nowhere in sight.

Yelling out her name, Mary rushed into the bed-room.
The famed flier laid motionless in her bed. The face that

once lit up rooms as she entered was now covered in dry red blood, coming from her nose and mouth.

"Dear God! What a shame!" cried Mary. She covered Helen's face with the bed sheet as Mr. Wright wiped his eyes.

Newspapers throughout the country carried the news of the pioneer aviatrix's death. An autopsy was performed on January 8, 1947 by a New York doctor at the Bellevue Hospital morgue. However, he failed to determine the cause of death. When I interviewed Helen's niece, Amy Lannan, in 2006 for the Helen Richey documentary that I was developing, she told me that the Richey family never received the autopsy report. They received Helen's body a week after her death and held her funeral at the Hunter-Edmundson-Shriffler Funeral home, followed by a precession to the McKeesport Cemetery.

Helen Richey's death has never been questioned until now. Might it have been that she knew way too many sensitive details that didn't need to be released . . . EVER?

Chapter 19

Last One Standing

Hats off to the ladies of the Golden Age of Aviation! As the years went by they continued to challenge the wind. Many died in the process—Harriet Quimby, Bessie Coleman, Amelia Earhart, and Frances Marsalis to name a few.

Several of the women who joined the Woman's Air Service Pilots 318th lost their lives during ferrying assignments—such as Margaret Oldenburg, Helen Jo Severson, Jane Champlin Kathryn Lawrence, Elizabeth Erickson, Marjorie Edwards, Margie Davis, and Clara Kay Portzline. But that didn't stop others like Jacqueline (Jackie) Cochran whose determination brought her even more recognition. After all she was the only pilot who consistently maintained the spotlight. Others found their own niches, such as instructing future pilots, working within the aircraft industry as a designer or consultant, writing books or manuals on the subject of aviation's past and leading up to its future opportunities.

The American public, both men and woman, were depending upon air travel more than ever before as the

1950's began to take shape. Even though the United States was not physically at war, the Cold War was indeed a major threat. However, for Jackie Cochran life was an opportunity for bravura. She received honors, awards, and more publicity than ever before in her career as a pilot. She was the last familiar aviation legend around and a series of honors were bestowed upon her for perhaps for that very reason: the Distinguished Flying Cross, the Distinguished Service Metal, the French Legion for Honor, the Florida's Distinguished Women Citizens Metal, and promotion to Colonel in the United States Air Force. Where Earhart and Richey left off, Jackie Cochran was front and center.

Liberty Magazine approached her to write several articles in upcoming additions dealing with foreign correspondents. Never completing high school she was apprehensive about accepting. However, once she was guaranteed that a staff member would revise her notes, she quickly agreed. Or, did she have an ulterior motive for needing those journalistic credentials?

Always wanting to get to the Pacific Theater where the United States had battled Japan, she contacted her old advocate General 'Hap' Arnold to issue her military orders as a Special Consultant. That was the access she needed in order to officially visit Japan. Of course this would give her the occasion to fly over the mandates Earhart flew over back before the war in the Pacific. Jackie wasn't going to let that prospect get away. She even made a public relations ploy by stopping on a few islands to interview the soldiers stationed there. At Tinian Island she interviewed a few professional baseball players who staged exhibition games for military personnel. Her plane was in the area so why not kill two birds with one stone?

The most startling revelation was her visit to the Japanese Imperial Palace where she viewed files on Amelia Earhart. No other person, yet alone a woman, had access to the Palace. But Jackie informed the staff that she wanted to interview Japanese woman fliers, which the Japanese had as well as the Chinese. Whatever did she read in the files with Earhart's name on them? Better yet, what happened to them? Could that have been the reason she was offered the job as foreign correspondent in the first place?

Jackie wasn't the only one visiting the islands to seek information after the war. George Putnam was on his own mission. He wanted answers as well. Perhaps Jackie wasn't to share her information with him. So he took matters into his own hands by contacting his old acquaintance, Vincent Astor who just happened to own a very large yacht. This is exactly what George needed to make his own trip down to the island of Saipan. He set out to conduct his own investigation as to what happened to Amelia and Fred. Disappointed that he was unable to find out anything at all, he realized he was too late and returned to California.

As the United States entered into the Korean War, the Pacific Ocean became off limits to civilians. It wasn't until the early 1960's that the mystery of the disappear-ance of Amelia Earhart began to surface once again. With all the problems in the Far East now concluded, could the greatest mystery of the 1937 World Flight possibly be solved?

Chapter 20

Renewed Interest

The first glimmer of revisiting the 1937 mystery of what happened Earhart and Noonan came when a CBS radio broadcaster named Fred Goerner of San Francisco, California, interviewed Josephine Akiyama. In an article that appeared in the *San Mateo Times* she told her story of seeing a plane fall from the sky. A white woman with short hair and a man who had hurt his head (she could see the blood) were quickly seized from the plane. Japanese soldiers accompanied them both to the Japanese command center on the island of Saipan. Goener was so fascinated after reading her story that he brought her on his radio station to interview her for his audience members.

Josephine Akiyama explained that in the summer of 1937 she was eleven years old and riding her bicycle down to the Tanapag Harbor to deliver lunch to her brother-in-law who worked at a secret seaplane base. On her way she heard a plane overhead. Ten minutes later she noted a group of people gathered near the harbor. A tall white woman and a man were surrounded by the natives and Japanese soldiers who lead the two to a building known as the Japanese Headquarters. She didn't see the man or woman leave the building. From that moment on Goerner spent the next several years investigating her story. His book, *The Search for Amelia Earhart* was written in 1966 and takes the reader along as he explores the Marshall Islands, Mili atoll, and Saipan.

He encountered Admiral Chester Nimitz who said, "You're onto something that will stagger your imagination." Goerner believed he had the opportunity to uncover something monumental. Discouraging moments did occurred during his investigations, however. At one point, after spending hours diving into Tanapag Harbor, he thought he had discovered a part of the Electra. After it was examined by aviation experts, however, the part was determined to have originated from a Japanese 'Bettsy' aircraft.

Just when he was ready to give up Goerner decided to travel to Washington, D.C. to arrange a few interviews with government personnel on the disap-pearance of the pair of aviators. Admiral Nimitz contacted Goerner by phone to inform him that Earhart and Noonan did indeed go down in the Marshall Islands and were picked up by the Japanese soldiers.

One person who could hardly wait to have the opportunity to revisit Saipan after the war was Thomas Devine. He was a young soldier stationed on Saipan in 1944 when an Okinawan woman showed him the grave sites of Earhart and Noonan. Devine tried several times after the war to revisit Saipan, but was never able to obtain clearance for his return. His objective was to continue his investigations of those grave sites. Devine had his own strategy to obtain the truth, or at least prove Earhart and Noonan did indeed arrive on the island of Saipan. The only stumbling block was the evidence.

For years his visit to Saipan was denied. Finally in 1963 the long awaited authorization arrived in his mailbox. He was determined to locate the burial site even though it nearly nineteen years had passed. The previously neatly kept cemetery was now a full grown deteriorating grassy lot. An even bigger problem was going to be acquiring the permission he needed to excavate the grave sites from the government officials on Saipan. If indeed, there were any remains to unearth in the first place. Thomas Devine never gave up his search for answers to the disappearance of Earhart and Noonan.

In Devine's 1987 book, *The Amelia Earhart Incident*, he details his personal visit to Mrs. Morrissey (Amelia's younger sister) who spent forty years of her life searching for answers from President Roosevelt, government officials, military personnel, media, and anyone who could or would confirm the truth behind the World Flight and what happened to Amelia and Fred. Just like the Helen Richey's family, Amelia's family appeared to accept what they were TOLD. However, their hearts knew there might be a far different version of their loved ones' deaths. In the dictionary the word TRUST precedes TRUTH. Does that make sense?

One summer day in 1961 Devine went to visit Mrs. Morrissey at her home in West Bedford, Massachusetts. That visit changed his life forever. He saw men wearing white shirts and black suits lurking near a black car parked in front of Mrs. Morrissey's home. Devine's all-inclusive analysis is priceless research to anyone examining the disappearance theory. Even more astonishing was his foresight to publish an ad in a military-based magazine called *The Leatherneck*. Devine requested anyone with any information whatsoever regarding Earhart's mission to get in touch with him directly. Because he included his address in the ad, he was seriously confident that someone would respond. His hope became a reality when several prospects came forward with their experiences on Saipan. Henry Duda, Robert Wallack, and Earsken Nabers contacted him to provide Devine with the evidence that he needed to confirm Earhart, Noonan, and the Electra surfaced on before Saipan before World War II. All of this is detailed in his book.

More investigators came forth during the mid-1960s, such as Joe Gervais and Robert Dinger. The two Air Force pilots were stationed on the island of Okinawa and created a report called "Operation Earhart," which Gervais later detailed in his book, *Amelia Earhart Lives*, written with Joe Klaas in 1970 and revised in 2000.

Just by chance one day I called the operator to see if Joe Gervais had a phone number listed. Sure enough he did. I called immediately. To my surprise he answered his phone and welcomed my questions about his investigation of Amelia Earhart. By the second call, I ventured to ask his permission for me to interview him on film to add to the documentary I was producing titled, *Close To Closure*. To my amazement, Joe Gervais invited me to his home in Las Vegas to do the interview.

On March 26, 2003 I caught a plane to interview this outstanding gentleman. Gervais established the Amelia Earhart Society which is comprised of hundreds of researchers throughout the world who are actively searching for answers and evidence of this unsolved mystery, now nearly seventy-seventh years old.

One question I had on my mind going into the interview with Joe was what led him to conceived "Operation Earhart"? He explained that while stationed on Okinawa he was requested to fly New York Governor

Nelson Rockefeller, his daughter, and members of his staff on a six-day search for Rockefeller's missing son and companion in the early 1960's. They had been sailing through the Marshall Island when a storm had arisen causing their boat to capsize. Michael Rockefeller decided to swim to shore since it was only a mile and a half away. His body was never found. However, the body of his companion and the boat were.

Joe remembered Amelia Earhart had flown from New Guinea passing the same islands and she was never found. Since he didn't have any orders to return to Tokyo after completing his assignment pertaining to the search for Michael Rockefeller, he decided to fly toward New Guinea where Earhart and Noonan had dinner with fourteen people the evening before takeoff. He set out to contact each one of those fourteen individuals to question the state of affairs that long-ago night, which turned out to be Amelia and Fred's last supper.

At that time, Gervais could locate only one remain-ing person who attended that dinner. The other thirteen had relocated all over the world, and he spent years tracking them down. Nevertheless, that one person reported firsthand information that convinced Joe there was more involved with the World Flight than just Earhart topping off her career in 1937. The gentleman remembered the Electra was guarded by heavily armed military soldiers as soon as it landed. No one was permitted to get near it from the moment it landed until the moment both Earhart and Noonan boarded it for takeoff.

Upon his retirement from the United States Air Force, Joe focused full-time on furthering his investigation. He teamed up with Joe Klaas, a writer from California, and during the next two decades they spent their own money following up every possible lead: from Earhart's survival, rescue, deprograming, and new identity as Irene Craigmile-Bolam (she married in 1958).

Gervais and Klaas swore they had found Amelia Earhart. A legal battle followed by Irene Bolam verses McGraw-Hill, the publisher of their book, *Amelia Earhart Lives*. The suit was in the amount of one million dollars. When requested by the Gervais and Klaas' attorney to provide proof that Irene Bolam was not Earhart by having her be fingerprinted . . . she refused! Her one million dollar lawsuit was dropped. The question remains . . . why did Irene Bolam refuse to be finger printed?

Author Elgin Long and his wife Marie released their book in 2001: *Amelia Earhart: The Mystery Solved*. They claimed through their extensive calculations, to have the correct latitude and longitude of the Electra at the time of its decent into the depths of the Pacific Ocean. Better known as the "Crash and Sink" theory, Long has spent millions of dollars throughout the years searching for that exact spot. The line of position 157-337 has been examined, as well as every other possible site in that area, with no results to date. Weather conditions definitely change the ocean floor over the decades. If there had been wreckage from the Electra, it would probably be safe to say it could now be hundreds if not thousands of miles away.

I had made several trips to Atchison, Kansas during the Amelia Earhart Festival which takes place during the third weekend in July. It is a two-day celebration of her life filled with tours of the Earhart family home, breakfast with the authors (past and present of books written about her career), lectures, award dinner, private parties, fireworks, and so forth. The Chamber of Commerce welcomes and honors their native daughter through this celebration which has been ongoing for nearly twenty years. My experience involved interviewing fans, family, authors, and researchers to produce the documentary, *Close To Closure: The Amelia Earhart Mystery*, which had its debut during the festival in 2007.

My interview with David Bowman took place in 2005 he brought his just published book, *Legerdemain*, to the Festival breakfast with the authors. He had extensive research on the ITASCA radio transmissions. He interviewed David Bellarts, the son of Chief Radioman Leo Bellarts who was stationed on the ITASCA on July 2, 1937. Bowman received a copy of the logs of radio activity from David Bellarts that were in the Bellarts family's possession since 1937. The original logs were donated to the national archives in Washington, D.C. in 1974.

In chapter sixteen of his book, Bowman gives a detailed breakdown of each transmission and its relevance during those nail-biting moments aboard the Electra as Amelia was screaming into the microphone to deaf ears.

Since our meeting in 2005, David and I stayed in contact as I kept him up to speed on the finishing touches of my documentary. I informed him of receiving a letter which was going to be presented in the film. Several researchers knew of this letter, but didn't know who had received it from Mrs. Ann Devine.

The letter was written by Art Beech of Grey Bull, Wyoming on August 10, 2003 and sent to Thomas Devine's home. At that time Devine was very ill which was one of the reasons he didn't want to go on film then. So we spent many evenings talking about his investigations. Unfortunately he passed away several weeks later. The good thing was that Tom was able to receive Art Beech's letter in time. I'm sure it gave Tom a great deal of satisfaction. Mrs. Devine sent it to me, along with the original photo of the Okinawan lady, Tom in his uniform at the grave site on Saipan, and the jail that Amelia and Fred were taken to upon their capture.

When David told me of his upcoming revision of *Legerdemain* in 2007, I suggested he go ahead and add Art Beech's letter which explained that his uncle (John H. Nichols) was an eyewitness to Earhart's plane being flown to the hanger in which it was set on fire, then bulldozed into a pile with other demolished Japanese planes. To find any part of the Electra would be like looking for a needle in a haystack. That could support the reason why Fred Goener couldn't find a piece of Earhart's plane.

The revision is an excellent reference book for any Amelia Earhart researcher to have in their library. Facts and evidence surrounding the disappearance of Ameila Earhart and her navigator Fred Noonan will be lost if researchers should ever halt their desire to search out the TRUTH!

Chapter 21

The ITASCA
by
David K. Bowman

A critical component in the mystery of Amelia Earhart is the events on the ITASCA, both reported and unreported. Some of them have only been published in recent years in an article entitled, "KHAQQ Calling ITASCA" by David K. Bowman and David Bellarts. When they are all considered, one gains greater perspective but is also faced with new mysteries.

Significant elements include the following:

Regarding radio communication with Lae, Chief Leo Bellarts, the lead radio operator aboard the ITASCA, reported that "We had no contact between the ITASCA and Lae, New Guinea. We couldn't work that distance, their frequencies were different than ours, and we didn't pay any attention to Lae. We figured we would be briefed through the regular channels." Further briefing, of course, was not forthcoming, as it appears that each of the services involved, the Army Air Force, the navy and the coast guard, were not fully aware of what the other was doing. Communication was dismal between the services, which may not have been completely coincidental, as orchestrated partial information was a favored technique of FDR.

FDR was noted for having one service handle his incoming communications and one service handle his outgoing communications. In that way, nobody had a full picture of FDR's activities. David Horner, in his recent book, *The Earhart Enigma*, referred to the above situation as a series of concurrent black operations. And indeed, that may be close to the truth and is a key new perspective that has surfaced in recent years.

Regarding the reception of Earhart's voice, Chief Bellarts remarked in a long ago interview with Elgin Long that "The last time we heard her voice it was so loud and clear that you could hear her outside the radio shack. She was so loud that I ran up to the bridge expecting to see her coming in for a landing." Earhart's signal strength was an S5, the highest signal strength. "We heard her quite a few times, but that last time, it sounded as if she would have broken out in a scream if she hadn't stopped talking. She was just about ready to break into tears and go into hysterics, that's exactly the way I'd describe her voice, I'll never forget it." Aside from Earhart's emotional status, this report raises another problem. In light of strong evidence that Earhart ditched in the Marshall Islands, one is faced with a new dilemma. How could Earhart have come within almost visual distance of the ITASCA and then, within one to two hours splash down in the Marshalls—some 800 miles distant?

One possible answer is a phenomenon called signal bouncing, which makes a radio signal seem to be coming from a point closer than it really is. Although Chief Bellarts was very insistent year later that signal bouncing was not occurring, it is the only viable solution to the above puzzle.

Earhart's radio usage practices also present a mystery, as personnel on the ITASCA all felt she should have known better, and were left puzzled and aggravated. "During the flight, the ITASCA radio operators were getting disgusted with her for not staying on schedule and just hanging up after just a few words. She apparently didn't listen for us at all. She'd call, come on and just say, the weather's overcast and then just hang it up, not go ahead. She never tried to establish contact until the last—the last quart of gas she had. We could have gotten her on 500 KCS—all she had to do is hold down the key and we could have taken a bearing on her from the ship's directional finder."

On the surface, it appears inexplicable why Earhart made it impossible for anyone to get a bearing on her other than because of her ineptitude. But there is one explanation for this puzzle which some researchers have considered and that is that *Earhart did not want anyone to know her bearing as a matter of security*. In other words, Earhart's defying attempts at locating her may have been necessary because locating her would have destroyed a covert operation.

Could that have been the reason for seemingly incompetent radio practice?

It is significant that the weather on and near Howland Island that day was reasonably benevolent. "There were puffy clouds to the Northwest but plenty of blue in between them. Other than that, it was a very clear day. The prevailing winds were easterly, toward Howland Island." So the weather shouldn't have turned Earhart back or caused her any trouble. And yet, Rollin Reineck reported in his 2003 book, *Amelia Earhart Survived*, that he had found a U.S. Army Air Force G-2 (intelligence) memorandum that reported the Army Air Force heard Earhart state over the radio after her apparent approach to Howland that she was turning north. The memorandum, which is shown in Reineck's book, did not state which radio station picked up this broadcast, although it may well have been the radio set used on Howland by the colonists.

The Army Air Force G-2 memorandum may well be a confirmation of the operation run by FDR which was suggested at the beginning of this chapter. The memorandum also suggests that Earhart was indeed involved in the covert operation, in which the Army Air Force was acting as her control. It also seems to confirm that the coast guard and navy were being kept out of the loop by Army Air Force intelligence.

Further corroboration of the above is given in an interview of Earhart's secretary Margot DeCarie by journalist Frederick Goerner in the 1960s. In his book, *The Search for Amelia Earhart*, Goerner made it seem that the below interview was with Earhart's temporary secretary Vivia Maatta, but it turned out later that Goerner was simply trying to give DeCarie some anonymity by camouflaging the interview's source. One wonders what Ms. Maatta must have thought about this charade.

At the beginning of the interview, DeCarie nervously said, "I promised secrecy" to Goerner over the telephone. "But I'll tell you this," she ventured, "if Eugene Vidal was still living, he could tell you all you'll ever want to know. I used to pick him up and drive him around when he came to Burbank from Washington. He made several trips during the period when the plane was being rebuilt."

"What was unusual about that?" Goerner asked.

"I'll ask you a couple of questions, and you can draw your own conclusions", DeCarie responded. "First, do you really think Purdue University bought that plane for Amelia [Earhart's Electra] and do you think that it was intended for some kind of vague experimentation? Second, if the whole thing was a publicity stunt, as a lot of people seem to think, why did the government assign some of its top experts to the flight [Clarence Kelly Johnson] and why did President Roosevelt have an airfield [Howland Island] built for her? Last, do you believe the President ordered the Navy to spend $4 million [$60 million in current dollars] on a search for a couple of stunt fliers?"

"Won't you tell me what *you* think?" Goerner then asked.

Startlingly, the secretary said, "Only this. President Roosevelt knew about everything. He knew the price Amelia paid."

"Don't you feel it's about time Amelia received some justice," Goerner asked.

"When one does the things Amelia was doing, one can't expect to receive justice. She knew that. She talked to me."

"Do you think there's any possibility Amelia is still alive?" Goerner then asked.

"She's dead. She died a long time ago. If she had survived the war, she would have come home even if she had to swim," the secretary said.

"Do you think the Japanese captured her?" Goerner continued.

"Of course they did," the secretary said flatly.

"Where?"

"All I can tell you is it was within moderate range of Howland Island"

"Did she intend to land at Howland?"

"In the beginning she did."

"Beginning of what?"

"I mean that was her intention after the first change of plans, but before what really happened."

"I'm sorry. I don't understand."

"That's all I'm going to say. I've already said too much."

The above suggests that there was a control available on a certain classified frequency, or how else could the plans have been changed so quickly and at the last moment? And as previously mentioned it appears that the control for the covert operation may well have been the Army Air Force.

Another telling issue was the large number of resident birds reported on Howland Island. According to Chief Bellarts, "We went ashore and killed hundreds of them. The reason was the concern that they might fly into the propellers of Earhart's plane."

Interestingly, Lieutenant Cooper of the U.S. Army, who was tasked to survey Howland before Earhart's arrival, later indicated privately that given both the high bird population and the crude condition of the landing strip, he couldn't believe Earhart had seriously intended to land there. Radioman O'Hare also stated in a later interview with Frederick Goerner that *he* doubted that Earhart ever seriously intended to land on Howland. However, O'Hare never stated his reasons for his belief, at least not publicly.

In addition, the government had ordered the ITASCA to generate a thick smoke screen to guide Earhart in to the island. According to Chief Bellarts, "I was actually on the bridge at the time and overheard them say, 'Make smoke.' I tell you when they make smoke they can lay down a smoke screen like you can't believe." If Earhart was actually that close to Howland, then she should have seen the smokescreen. The inference was that Earhart was actually not that close to Howland, which would seem to corroborate that signal bouncing was at work, thus making Earhart seem closer than she actually was.

Another point of interest was the inability of the other two ships assigned to guide in Earhart, to even receive her broadcasts. The USS ONTARIO, a weather ship stationed halfway between Lae and Howland, was supposed to send out N's in Morse code on 400 KC's for Earhart to home in on. The ONTARIO didn't hear Earhart because her ability to transmit in the lower frequency range was nonexistent, due to her not taking her trailing antenna with her. Overall, the radios on the ONTARIO could not operate above 500 KC nor receive above 3000 KCS. Since Earhart could not send below 3105 KCS, the ONTARIO's presence was a useless gesture

The U.S. Navy tug USS SWAN was stationed halfway between Howland and Hawaii. Earhart reportedly wanted the SWAN to transmit on 900 KC's at night and 9000 KC during the day, which was strange because the primary radio frequencies were to be 7500, 6210, 3105 and 500 KCS. The SWAN was thus also a pointless gesture because it had the same type of radios as the ONTARIO."

Of interest is that the ITASCA did have a direction finder aboard that operated at 500 KCS or lower. But it could not receive any of Earhart's transmissions at 3105 or 6210 KCS, thus rendering it useless. Said Bellarts, "I went up to the bridge just for insurance to operate the D/F. We had no idea in the world that she couldn't use 500 KC. So I went up there and started it up and was standing by just in case. I was right there and if she'd come in I'd have her in 30 seconds. Actually, that D/F was my pride and joy because I've had an awful lot of experience on the ship board type. Earhart was not alerted to the fact a special D/F had been set up aboard the ITASCA. No D/F was aboard during her flight that would cover her frequency of 3105 or 6210 KCS."

Another issue was the direction finder on Howland Island. It had been installed by Richard Black, a high level government employee and it has since come out that it was an experimental, classified device. Although if it was, the whole affair was handled badly, as RM2 Cipriani, who had been assigned to operate the unit, was given no training in its operation. It was a few days before Chief Bellarts discovered that Cipriani had inadvertently incorrectly operated the device, breaking the controlling cable early on in the effort to guide in Earhart. There was also some indication that the unit's battery may have run down during the early hours of 2 July 1937, in spite of efforts to keep it going with a battery from one of the ship's guns.

Regarding the gun battery, Chief Bellarts remarked cryptically, "I was not aware the batteries ran down during the night. In fact that is incorrect. Don't recall exactly which gun battery we used, but they were all OK until after she apparently 'went in.' Someone is guessing and they haven't guessed the correct answer, which will remain with me."

What could the answer have been?

Does the above indicate window dressing for a covert operation or a clumsy attempt at fooling the public into thinking Earhart was to receive close navigational help form multiple ships? Or could Earhart have just been careless in not informing the ITASCA that she was unable to transmit on 500 KCS? If that wasn't enough, Earhart reportedly left her communications notebook with Harry Balfour in Lae, so that she *couldn't* have followed her own pre-arranged procedures. Ultimately, the communi-cation arrangements for Earhart's last flight seem to have been either comically bad—or just window dressing.

Another controversial aspect of the ITASCA's efforts was their sending of "A's" in Morse code as a homing device. Bellarts said, "As for the length of time we sent "A's" on 7.5 megacycles [7500 KCS], we were advised that she wanted signals on the 7.5 frequency for her homing station. She apparently did not use them and I doubt that she even attempted." Where the controversy entered was the assertion of at least one researcher that the ITASCA sent A's so profusely that Earhart couldn't get through by voice. This assertion seems to have no real basis in fact.

The key documentation of radio assignment on the ITASCA was a copy of a duty assignment memorandum issued by Chief Bellarts' division officer, Lieutenant W. L. Sutter. According to the document, Chief Bellarts had been assigned responsibility for monitoring all incoming transmissions from Earhart's plane. Radioman Third Class (RM3) C. O'Hare was assigned to handle all other radio traffic received by the ITASCA. RM3 W. L. Galten was assigned to man the ship's direction finder when Earhart's aircraft came within 1000 miles of Howland Island. RM3 G. E. Thompson was the relief operator for all three of the above operators. Radioman Second Class (RM2) Frank Cipriani was assigned to operate the direction finder on Howland Island.

Additionally, David Bellarts supplied a copy of the radio activity logs from the ITASCA relating to Earhart's flight from 1900 (7:00 p.m.) Howland Island Time, on July 1, 1937 through 1039 (10:39 a.m.) the next day, July 2, 1937. Over the years, the ship's radio log has been the subject of controversy, partially because its completeness and accuracy have been in doubt, and partially because of the heavy abbreviations in the log, which are confusing. Initially, Chief Bellarts expected to be called to testify at an official inquiry, but that never happened. As a result, his copy of the log, the original, remained in the keeping of the Bellarts family from 1937 until 1974, when they donated it to the national archives. David maintains that the family copy has not been altered in any way.

What follows is a transcript of Earhart-related radio traffic starting early 2 July 1937. For clarity, I have inserted a translation to plain language below each entry, in italics.

0400   EARHART HEARD FONE / WILL LISTEN ON HOUR AND HALF ON 3105-SEZ SHE BROADCAST WEATHER FONE 3105

Earhart heard via phone (voice). She said she will listen on the hour and half hour on 3105 kilocycles. She broadcast the weather by voice on 3105 kilocycles.

0453   HEARD EARHART (PART CLDY)

Heard Earhart, saying "Partly Cloudy."

0614   WANTS BEARING ON 3105 KCS // ON HOUR // WILL WHISTLE IN MIC

*Earhart wants bearing on 3105 kilocycles on the hour. She will whistle in **microphone**.*

0615   ABOUT TWO HUNDRED MILES OUT // APPX // WHISTLING // NW

About 200 miles out from Howland, approximately. Whistling in the microphone.

Coming from the northwest.

0645 PSE TAKE BEARING ON US AND REPORT IN HALF HOUR

Please take a bearing on us and report in half an hour.

0646 I WILL MAKE A NOISE IN MIC – ABT 100 MILES OUT

I will make a noise in microphone. Am about 100 miles out from Howland Island.

0742 KHAQQ CLNG ITASCA WE MUST BE ON YOU BUT CANNOT SEE U BUT GAS IS RUNNING LOW BEEN UNABLE TO REACH YOU BY RADIO WE ARE FLYING AT A 1000 FT

KHAQQ calling ITASCA. We must be on you but cannot see you but gas is running low. Been unable to reach you by radio. We are flying at 1000 feet.

0754 KHAQQ CLNG TASCA WE ARE CIRCLINGBUT CANNOT HR U

KHAQQ calling ITASCA. We are circling but cannot hear you.

0800 KHAQQ CLNG ITASCA WE RECD UR SIGS BUT UNABLE TO GET A MINIMUM. PSE TAKE BEARING ON US AND ANS 3105 WID VOICE.

KHAQQ calling ITASCA. We received your
signals but are unable to get a minimum.
Please take a bearing on us and answer on
3105 kilocycles in voice.

0843   KHAQQ TO ITASCA. WE ARE ON THE LINE 157
337. WL REPT MSG. WE WL REPT THIS ON
6210 KCS WAIT. WE ARE RUNNING ON LINE
LSNIN 6210 KCS.

KHAQQ to ITASCA. We are on the line 157-
337. Will repeat message. We will repeat this
on 6210 kilocycles wait. We are running on
line, listening on 6210 kilocycles.

Chief Bellarts was on duty during the entire period
that transmissions were received from Earhart's plane,
which was from 0205 (2:05 a.m.) until 0800 (8:00 a.m.)
July 2, 1937. He was not compelled to stand such a long
watch, but insisted upon it out of a conscientious desire
to personally be there.

Starting shortly before 7:00 p.m. July 1, 1937,
according to the log, weak, unreadable signals began
coming through. The following entries regarding Earhart's
transmissions indicate what began to happen early on 2
July 1937. As in the previous transcript, I have inserted a
translation to plain language below each entry, in italics.

Chief Bellarts' radio log:

What follows next is the log compiled by RM3 Galten
and RM3 O'Hare, who operated the onboard direction
finder during the same period that Chief Bellarts was

manning the radio. According to their entries, they monitored several frequencies, which included 500 kilocycles, 3205 kilocycles, 6210 kilocycles, and 7500 kilocycles. Another thing that was noted was that the men operating the direction finder also logged in messages they were receiving from another party or parties. The messages were generally inquiries as to the status of the flight, but it is not clear from the log whom they were from. I have included them where they are relevant to clarification, preceded by the letter "Q" for query. The reader should note that at the beginning of the log, RM3 Galten was on the watch. RM3 O'Hare relieved him at 0200. At 1033 hours RM3 Galten relieved O'Hare.

Direction finder log:

0400   Q: HAVE U ESTABLISHED CONTACT WITH PLANE YET
HRD HER BUT DNT KNW IF SHE HRS US YET.
GAVE WX TO EARHART ON FONE 3105.

Q: Have you established contact with the plane yet?
Heard her but don't know if she hears us yet.
Gave weather to Earhart by voice on 3105 kilocycles.

0440   Q: U HR EARHART ON 3105
YES BUT CAN'T MAKE HER OUT

Q: Do you hear Earhart on 3105 kilocycles?
Yes, but I can't make her out.

0455   EARHART BROKE IN ON FONE 3105 / NW????
UNREADABLE

Earhart broke in by voice on 3105 kilocycles. From the northwest? Signal unreadable.

0740   EARHART ON NW SEZ RUNNING OUT OF GAS ONLY ½ HR LEFT CANT HR US AT ALL. WE HR HER AND ARE SENDING ON 3105 ES 500 SAME TIME CONSTANTLY AND LISTENING IN FER ER FREQUENTLY.

Earhart on (?). She says she is running out of gas and has only a half hour left. She can't hear us at all. We hear her and are sending on 3105 kilocycles and 500 kilocycles at the same time constantly, and listening in for her frequently.

0857   AMELIA ON AGN AT 0800 SEZ HRG US ON 7.5 MEGS CA. STILL SENDING ON 7500 KCS TELLING HER TO CA ON 3105 AND SENDING OUT SIGS FER HER TO OBSERVE BEARINGS ON. MAINTAINING LISTENING WATCH 3105 KCS 7500 ES 500.

Amelia on again at 0800. She says she is hearing us on 7.5 megacycles calling. Still sending on 7500 kilocycles telling her to call on 3105 and sending out signals for her to observe bearings on. Maintaining a listening watch on 3105 kilocycles, 7500 kilocycles and 500 kilocycles.

In between the above entries were numerous remarks indicating:

- Transmissions by ITASCA in attempted response to Earhart's received transmissions
- Transmissions by ITASCA in an attempt to contact and get an acknowledgment from Earhart
- Routine indications that no transmissions had been received from Earhart
- Lists of frequencies on which Bellarts was listening, which were 500 KCS, 3205 KCS and 6210 KCS

The foregoing material came from records held by the Bellarts family and seems to be above question as to its accuracy. David Bellarts maintains that his father was not a party to any alteration of this radio log. If readers have any doubts, they can look at reproductions of the original to see for themselves. A major point of reference for investigators, the ITASCA radio log was initially only released to the media or cited in fragments. It wasn't until 1987 that a complete copy of the ITASCA radio log was finally released.

Although the above cited radio log material from Chief Bellarts' family seems totally reliable, the other two important records maintained by ITASCA, the ITASCA deck log and the Howland Island Detachment radio log have been found to be far more questionable.

In an extensive article in *Naval History Magazine*, John P. Riley Jr. asserted that the deck log of the ITASCA had been partially falsified and that the Howland Island detachment radio log was almost completely bogus. Riley concluded this from the accounts of radio operators Yau Fai Lum and Ah Kin Leong who were assigned to the Howland Island radio station.

Mr. Riley first wondered if the Howland log might be fictitious, when he showed Lum copies of the Howland log indicating that Lum had stood radio watches on the direction finder on Earhart's frequency along with Radioman 2nd Class Frank Cipriani. Lum firmly maintained that those entries were completely fictitious and that he had neither stood such watches, nor worked with Cipriani. The other radio operators were Henry Lau (since deceased) and Ah Kim Leong. When asked what he knew about the situation, Leong declared in a September 4, 1994 letter to Riley:

"No idea who wrote the false log. I stand no radio watch on Howland Island. Cipriani, Henry Lau, and me was on the Coast Guard Cutter Itasca when it left Howland Island looking for Earhart."

Evidence, which Riley thought further supports the thesis that the Howland log was falsified, is the frequent misspelling of Lum's name as "Yat Fai Lum." "I should know how to spell my own name," Lum stated.

Overall, Riley felt that Lum and Leong were sincere and their stories merited more credence than the ITASCA documents, because both men had demonstrable integrity and neither man had any discernible motive to fabricate logs.

But here, we encounter another mystery in the Earhart disappearance: Chief Bellarts definitely made it clear to his family that Cipriani was not ordered aboard the ITASCA by Commander Thompson before the ship left to search for Earhart. Dave Bellarts is adamant about this point. Dave also was emphatic that he didn't think Commander Thompson would jeopardize his reputation and career by falsifying the ship's log or any other record.

What's the answer?

Dave Bellarts offered another piece of information regarding what happened on July 2, 1937. According to his father, there were no visibility problems over most of Howland Island that day, which is contrary to some assertions that the main reason Earhart didn't or couldn't successfully land on Howland Island was excessive cloud cover. At the moment, this contradiction remains unexplained, although this writer is inclined to believe the report of Chief Bellarts, or that perhaps the glare of the morning sun on the sea near Howland Island might have caused Earhart's visibility difficulties.

Still another piece of information that David Bellarts revealed is regarding the new direction finder operated on Howland Island by radioman Cipriani. According to Chief Bellarts, the direction finder was operated by rotating a wheel-like device from side to side in an oscillating pattern to try to determine the direction of a radio signal. The oscillating movement was necessary because there was a wire attached to the underside of the wheel, which would break if the wheel was rotated continuously in either direction. Chief Bellarts later told his family that the direction finder had been disabled during its use on Howland Island, when the operator, Cipriani, rotated the wheel continuously without stopping. The damage wasn't discovered until shortly after the ITASCA had returned to Howland Island. At that time, the direction finder was brought aboard the ship and Chief Bellarts dismantled and inspected the unit. He found the broken wire and discovered that the device's battery had failed during Earhart's flight due to over-loading or running dry. Note earlier cited comments by Chief Bellarts denying that a batter had failed. Another conundrum.

After repairing the unit, Chief Bellarts said nothing about it, according to David, because he knew that

Cipriani hadn't received training for operating the device and it would have served no purpose to get him into trouble. As a result, it now appears that even when the direction finder's battery was good, the unit was inoperative. One has to conclude that due to a series of errors and oversights, the deck was stacked against Amelia Earhart.

David Bellarts provided yet another piece of striking information regarding the ITASCA. According to him, his father noticed during Earhart's attempted flight to Howland that documents were disappearing frequently from the "radio shack", the compartment used on the ship for radio activity. He reported this, and in short order the executive officer, second in command of the ITASCA, immediately ordered Bellarts to secure under lock and key all papers relating to Earhart's flight. According to Dave, his father suspected a particular ITASCA crewmember of the thefts, but was never able to secure incontrovertible proof.

As result, we now have yet a couple of other side mysteries in the disappearance of Amelia Earhart. Who was taking official documents from the ITASCA's radio shack—and why? And was Radioman Cipriani on Howland Island or the ITASCA?

Another issue relating to the ITASCA is Morgenthau Transcript. One of the most compelling pieces of evidence of government involvement in Amelia Earhart's last flight and her disappearance, the Morgenthau Transcript is a transcript of a phone conversation between Secretary of the Treasury Morgenthau and Malvina Scheider, Eleanor Roosevelt's secretary.

This document was first published in *My Courageous Sister* by Muriel Earhart Morrissey and Carol Osborne. That, in itself, is amazing, since Muriel Morrissey maintained publicly that her sister had not been flying a secret mission for the government. Be that as it may, the document is located in the Morgenthau Collection in the Franklin Roosevelt Presidential Library in Hyde Park, NY.

Henry Morgenthau was Secretary of the Treasury in 1937 at the time of Earhart's disappearance, and one of his duties was oversight of the U.S. Coast Guard.

On April 26, 1938, Paul Mantz, who had been Earhart's technical advisor before her disappearance, wrote a letter to Eleanor Roosevelt, asking her to secure for him the "official report" of the Coast Guard cutter ITASCA in regard to Amelia Earhart's disappearance. Mantz indicated in his letter that he had already tried to get this report by requesting it from the Coast Guard and they had denied his request, indicating that *"the official report (log) could not be released except through certain channels"* (Emphasis is the author's). This last statement seems peculiarly evasive. Why should the government want to suppress the search report for a missing private pilot?

What Mantz wanted from the Coast Guard, in actuality, was a copy of the USCGC ITASCA radio log during the period of Earhart's disappearance.

The fact that government records regarding an ostensibly civilian flight were being withheld speaks volumes and indicates government involvement. Eleanor Roosevelt sent Mantz' letter to Morgenthau on May 10, 1938, along with a short note:

> A little while ago Floyd Odlum and his wife, Jacqueline Cochran, were at the White House when she received the Harmon Trophy for aviation. She told me they all felt that not enough search had been made amongst certain islands where Amelia might be. I told

her to send me a memo on the islands and the reasons why they felt this, and I would transmit it to you and to the Navy Department at once. Now comes this letter which is evidently inspired by Miss Cochran. I don't know whether you can send this man these records, but in any case, I am sending you the letter and let me know whatever your decision may be.

Affectionately E. R.

This short note speaks volumes. It is at once revelatory and cryptic. Not only does it indicate that there are records relating to Earhart's fate which the government is holding, it clearly indicates trepidation on Eleanor's part regarding releasing any of them to Paul Mantz. Mrs. Roosevelt seems to have definitely felt that the requested records would reveal things she would rather not reveal.

An additional document in the file of papers in the Franklin D. Roosevelt Library was a single sheet of paper with a few lines near the top, reading:

6/27
Sent to Mr. Morgenthau – Can he do this or what do I way [evidently a typo for "say"]? E.R.
Paul Mantz, Burbank, Calif. Wants Coast Guard data, which was originally turned over to him and he did not copy.

This document, like Eleanor's initial note to Morgenthau, is also revelatory as well as cryptic. "Can he do this or what do I say?" That remark clearly shows strong concern over Mantz' request for the ITASCA Report. And why was the document dated over a month after the Morgenthau Transcript? Was someone just late in making this note?

On May 13, 1938, Morgenthau made a telephone call to Malvina Scheider, to discuss Paul Mantz' request for information regarding the Earhart disappearance. The transcript of Morgenthau's end of the conversation remarkably was not removed from the files of material that were sent to the FDR Library in Hyde Park for public access. Morgenthau's staff evidently did not realize the import of the document.

"This letter that Mrs. Roosevelt wrote me about trying to get the report on Amelia Earhart. Now, I've been given a verbal report. If we're going to release this, it's just going to smear the whole reputation of Amelia Earhart, and my . . ." Morgenthau stated after exchanging the usual amenities with Malvina Scheider. He was interrupted at the end of the passage by a remark at the other end of the phone.

"Yes, but I mean if we give it to this man we've got to make it public; we can't let one man see it. And if we ever release the report of the ITASCA on Amelia Earhart, any reputation she's got is gone . . . ," Morgenthau continued.

"Now I know what Navy did and I know what the ITASCA did and I know how Amelia Earhart absolutely disregarded all orders, and if we ever release this thing, goodbye to Amelia Earhart's reputation," Morgenthau went on. "Now really—because if we give the access to one, we have to give it to all."

Morgenthau then expressed concern over the President's response to anyone in the public questioning the competence of the navy's and coast guard's search for Earhart.

"And we have the report of all those wireless messages and everything else, what that woman—happened to her the last few minutes. I hope I've just got to never make it public . . ." the transcript continued. "Well, still if she

[Eleanor] wants it, I'll tell her—I mean what happened. It isn't a very nice story."

Morgenthau concluded his conversation with Malvina Scheider oddly with the remarks: "Well, yes. There isn't anything additional to something like that. You think up a good one. Thank you."

Having concluded the phone conversation, Morgenthau then made several remarks to a Mr. Gibbons:

> "I mean we tried—people want us to search again those islands, after what we have gone through. You know the story, don't you?
>
> "We have evidence that the thing is all over, sure. Terrible. It would be awful to make it public."

The next day, May 14, 1938, Eleanor wrote a short note to Paul Mantz regarding his request:

> May 14, 1938
> My dear Mr. Mantz:
> I have made inquiries about the search which was made for Amelia Earhart and both the President and I are satisfied from the information which we have received that everything possible was done. We are sure that a very thorough search was made.
> Very sincerely yours,

This note seems premature, as there is at least no indication from the record that Morgenthau had decided what to do. In fact (see below) it wouldn't be until July 5, 1938 that Morgenthau would announce his decision to Eleanor.

Another interesting and enigmatic document, which appears in the file of material in the Franklin D. Roosevelt

Library, is an undated and unsigned note on White House stationery:

> Mr. Morgenthau says that he can't give out any more information than was given to the papers at the time of the search of Amelia Earhart.
>
> It seems they have confidential information which would completely ruin the reputation of Amelia and which he will tell you personally some time when you wish to hear it.
>
> He suggests writing this man and telling him that the President is satisfied from his information, and you are too, that everything possible was done.

Since it is unsigned and unaddressed, it is not completely clear to whom the note was written. However a careful reading of it indicates that it is probably to Eleanor Roosevelt from Henry Morgenthau's office. This document underscores the existence of unreleased information regarding Amelia Earhart.

The next document which appears on the record is a short note from Henry Morgenthau to Eleanor Roosevelt. The date "7-5" appears in the upper right hand corner. The note runs:

> Dear Eleanor:
>
> We have found it possible to send Mr. A. Paul Mantz a copy of the log of the ITASCA, which I think will supply him with all the data he asked for in his letter of June 21st.
>
> Sincerely,
>
> Henry

We have found it possible? What an interesting statement. It indicates that Morgenthau had perhaps hit upon a way of altering one of the documents in question so that it would be releasable to the public. This is certainly something that the community of Earhart researchers has been seriously considering of late.

The record continues with a note dated 7-5-38 from Eleanor to Morgenthau thanking him for finding it possible to send a copy of the log of the ITASCA to Paul Mantz. There seems to be about this short communication a sense of relief. Relief? One wonders why there should have been worry about releasing to the public a copy of a routine document.

Finally, there is a letter dated July 21, 1938 from RADM R. R. Wesche to Paul Mantz. The letter acknowledges Mantz' request and states that Wesche is pleased to forward the documents. The only puzzling thing is that the letter by Mantz which is referred to is dated June 21, 1938. Curiously, Mantz' letter to Eleanor was dated April 26, 1938 and there was no letter in the packet from the FDR Library dated June 21, 1938. Was the referenced date a typo or was there another letter from Mantz to Eleanor Roosevelt?

The first telling aspect was Morgenthau's repeated assertions that the "truth" about Amelia Earhart's disappearance would seriously damage her reputation. To what could he have been referring? The apprehension in her voice during her last transmissions?

Another thing is Morgenthau's remark, ". . . If we're going to release this, it's just going to smear the whole reputation of Amelia Earhart, and my . . ."

What did the ". . . and my . . . " refer to? Is it a subtle hint of trepidation on Morgenthau's part about his and the coast guard's handling of Earhart's support? Was Morgenthau about to say "and my reputation"?

Even more significant are Morgenthau's remarks about releasing the ITASCA report on Earhart's disappearance. A thorough review of the entire report indicates that the ITASCA's report is the furthest thing in the world from being hugely damaging to Earhart's reputation or memory. It is, in fact, fairly routine.

The inference, then, of Morgenthau's remark about the ITASCA report, is that there must have been another hitherto unrevealed report submitted by the commanding officer of the ITASCA, which was regarded as extremely sensitive.

Morgenthau next makes another remarkable statement regarding Earhart disregarding "all orders." This statement, from the lips of the Secretary of the Treasury, unquestionably proves that Earhart was flying for the U. S. Government on her second round-the-world attempt, and that there was more to Earhart's disappearance than was made public.

After some more mundane discussion, Morgenthau then makes yet another startling remark, when he refers to having received "the report of all those wireless messages and everything else." What could he have been referring to? The existing messages transmitted by Earhart that are recorded in the National Archive are relatively sparse and cryptic. The other messages sent between the coast guard, navy and federal government are relatively routine and far from damaging. And what did Morgenthau mean by "and everything else"? Again, we are left with a definite admission by the Secretary of the Treasury that there were additional message traffic and reports, which have never been made public.

Further, there is Morgenthau's remark, ". . . what that woman—happened to her the last few minutes. I hope I've just got to never make it public." What does he mean by it? Make what public? None of the message traffic reflects anything dramatic happening before Earhart disappeared, certainly nothing which would be a disaster if disclosed. Again, there is the clear impression that there was message traffic and other communications that were never released.

Overall, the Morgenthau Transcript both casts doubt on some assertions about what happened at Howland Island, and confirms others. What the transcript seems to conflict with is the contents of publicly released reports, with its remarks about unusual and embarrassing message traffic from ITASCA, as well as peril to Earhart's reputation if this information is released.

What the Morgenthau Transcript does confirm or lend credibility to, however, is the concept of a covert operation as suggested by the G-2 memorandum and Margot DeCarie's later remarks.

In the final analysis, the available data regarding Howland Island and the ITASCA seem to strongly corroborate that, instead of crashing into the sea near Howland Island during a purely commercial stunt flight, as the government has suggested, Amelia Earhart was on a covert flight for the government which went terribly awry.

What happened during the final hours of Earhart's flight, somewhere between Howland Island and the Marshall Islands, may be the key to the solution of this puzzling mystery.

Chapter 22

Amelia Earhart Birthplace Museum
by
Louise Foudray, Curator

Atchison, Kansas

As far back as 1840 the Otis residence played a paramount role in the beginning of Kansas history, as did the Missouri River, the Westward movements (of white ribbon covered wagons leaving Atchison and going west), the railroads and the struggles of wealth and progress spreading throughout Kansas. There are stories about the Underground Railroad and Amelia Earhart's grand-father Alfred G. Otis's part in helping the slaves cross the Missouri River and caring for them until they reached safety and created a new life.

Alfred G. Otis purchased several properties in the town of Atchison in 1860. One particular structure overlooking the Missouri River on the eastern side atop the river bank caught his eye. He decided to add onto the structure which had only three rooms. He enlarged the structure in 1873 since he and Mrs. Otis were planning on beginning a family in the near future. Several rooms were attached as well as an office where Mr. Otis and his law partner,

George W. Glick, began their law careers. Years later George Glick ran for Governor of Kansas and was elected in 1882, becoming the ninth man to hold that title.

Mr. and Mrs. Otis were the proud parents of two girls and four boys. Amy Otis (Amelia's mother) was a progressive person, traveling with her father, Judge Otis, and attending prestigious schools. She married Edwin Earhart five years after they met at her coming-out party when Amy was eighteen years old.

Amelia Earhart was born in her mother's bedroom at her grandparent's home in Atchison, Kansas in 1897. She lived with her parents in Kansas City, Kansas where Amelia's sister was born in 1899. Amelia would stay with her grandparents in Atchison during the school term to attend a private school, called the College Prepatory School, until she was twelve years old.

The Amelia Earhart Birthplace is the name of the family home today. The house itself tells a story that visitors can see, feel, and absorb. The story is about the childhood of one of the world's most famous women, her roots in Atchison, and the development of her vision, determination, and desire to accomplish. As one walks through the house, the spirit of Amelia Earhart is evident.

Amelia Earhart Birthplace Museum

In 1985 the Amelia Earhart Birthplace Museum was opened to visitors. At that time, however, very little restoration had been done. The prior owner was a physician who lived there with his family. When he passed away the property was up for sale. Many Atchison residents had a vision to return the home into a museum dedicating it to their hometown heroine, Amelia Earhart. Soon pictures, books, furniture, drapes, linen and so forth were secured as part of the task to restore the house back to how it looked in the early 1900's.

Quick forward to 1985: the insurance company holding the policy for the property said they would prefer the house have a full-time resident to protect the premises. Two different people agreed to live there. By 1987 the position was open again and the Board of Trustees asked me if I would be interested.

I was working twenty hours a week at the Atchison Library. My children were grown and living elsewhere, so I considered the position. I was used to caring for a fairly large home and informed the Board that I would try it for one year. Almost immediately I found that there were so many aspects of being the caretaker and historian that it became the epitome of multi-tasking. I read biographies of Amelia Earhart and discovered many things about this accomplished person to tell visitors. However, the problem at hand was to move into the designated rooms, clean the viewing rooms and be ready in two weeks for the Forest of Friendship celebration, including meeting the International 99's, accepting donated artifacts and welcoming all visitors with guided tours of the museum.

The years marched on and I am happy to say that 2014 will mark my twenty-seventh year affiliated with the Amelia Earhart Birthplace Museum. Many things have happened throughout my tenure: an increased number of visitors, completion of restoration projects, the on-going interest in all things dealing with Amelia Earhart, and the fascination of seeking to solve a mystery that seems never-ending.

The People I Have Met

Over the years I have met authors and researchers with fascinating stories to tell, such as the Sablan Family from Saipan Island and Sam Kahaluwa from Honolulu. I was able to attend several meetings in the founding days of the Amelia Earhart Society. Those were held at Purdue University, San Jose, Las Vegas, and Aspen. Some of us went to the Marshall Island for extended interviews and diving to view World War II airplanes left under the water. Joe Gervais, Bill Prymak, Ret. Capt. Gene Tissot, Joe Klass, Irene and John Bolam, Margaret Meade, and Pat Ward were some of the others, all skilled in their research of Amelia Earhart.

Muriel or "Pidge" Earhart-Morrissey (Amelia's sister) visited us for the last time in 1988. She was then eighty-eight years old. Muriel gave us information about the rooms that helped with the restoration process. We had lemonade in the main parlor and it was such a delight to hear her stories of their childhood here together.

Members of Amelia's family have come to Atchison during the festival weekend. Amy Morrissey-Kleppner, Amelia's niece, who resides in Vermont and is the closest relative living today, visited in 2003 and was interviewed for the documentary produced by Andrea Niapas titled, *Close To Closure: the Amelia Earhart Mystery*. The documentary was presented at the 2007 festival to a full house at the Atchison Theater. Another frequent visitor was George Putnam, Jr., Amelia's stepson, who recently died at the age of ninety-two. He, too, was interviewed and appeared in the documentary. Much of my time is spent contacting authors and researchers to be guests at our wonderful Amelia Earhart Festival.

Fay Gillis-Wells also visited Atchison several times each year. She was a charter member of the 99's organization of pilots. She told us Amelia was a quiet, private person but had an inner confidence and an intelligence that was greatly admired.

Sometimes the Responsibilities are Challenging but Rewarding

Here at the Amelia Earhart Birthplace Museum we are proud of our strong educational contribution to students, both locally and internationally. We furnish material on request, whether it concerns Amelia Earhart or Kansas. Recently I gave several interviews via telephone to the BBC in London. They expressed an immense interest in Amelia's career. In 1928 she became the first American woman to fly across the Atlantic Ocean with Wilmer Stultz and Slim Gordon aboard a plane called "The Friendship" which landed in Southampton, England. From that moment, the world was mesmerized with Amelia Earhart.

One memorable and rewarding event for me took place when Governor Sam Brownback extended an invitation to a small contingency of Atchison residences and museum representatives to travel to the State Capital building in Topeka to witness the installing of a plaque for Amelia Earhart in the "Walk of Honor" in front of the building.

As I reflect over my many years as caretaker and historian I am honored to be able to welcome visitors from every country. Their interest peeks as they move through the museum grasping first-hand where the most famous woman of the aviation world began her life. Amelia Earhart was the key that unlocked The Golden Age of Aviation.

Chapter 23

The Amelia Earhart Festival

The weekend closest to Amelia Earhart's birth date of July 24th kicks off the festival each year. In 1997 the first Amelia Earhart Festival took place, marking the 100th anniversary of Atchison's heroine's birth. The celebration is filled with events as follows:

- Aerobatic performers flying over the Missouri River.
- Birthday party for Amelia including a cake free to the public.
- Outdoor country music concert.
- 1 hour trolley tour of all Amelia Earhart sites throughout Atchison.
- Documentary films about Amelia's life shown at the theater.
- River side fireworks display set to music.
- The Amelia Earhart Pioneering Achievement Award Luncheon.

Over the years, increased numbers of Amelia Earhart researchers began to attend and soon formed a group with their own agenda. The Earhart Museum soon became the command center, and curator Louise Foundry welcomed each of them upon their arrival. Louise arranged their hotel reservations and transportation from the airport. Just about everyone hung around at the museum to discuss the latest investigations, and do a little sightseeing around Atchison until a program was designed by Louise. She was able to arrange an exciting weekend filled with the best of both worlds: plenty of fun and educational tourist activities, food and entertainment, as well as comradeship. As the program progressed, it soon was published into a brochure which would appear as follows:

- Friday
  A VIP Dinner:
  Old friends and new ones gather at a restaurant or
  the country club to enjoy good food and   .
  conversation.
- Saturday
  Breakfast with the Books:
  Begins at 9:00 a.m. at the Atchison Public Library
  where authors discuss their latest book with
  Amelia Earhart fans over delicious donuts and
  fresh coffee. Books can be purchased and
  signed by the authors.

Speakers' Symposium:

Beginning at 11:00 a.m. at the O'Malley-McAllister
Auditorium on the Benedictine College Campus.
Forum discussions on aviation as well as those
affiliated past and present.

Amelia Earhart Pioneering Achievement Award Luncheon:

Beginning at 12:30 p.m. on the Benedictine College Campus. An honoree is presented with a beautiful bust of Amelia Earhart as well as a $10,000.00 award for her work in the area of aviation as well as woman's advancements.

From 2:00 pm. to 5:30 p.m.

Free time to take in the sights of Atchison.

Perhaps a peaceful walk through Friendship Forest where you will be greeted by a life size bronze statue of Amelia Earhart. Then following a twisty windy pathway a top brinks bearing the names of women pilots (past and present) who were instrumental in our rich history of aviation. Winding around the beautiful scenic park under a warm sunny afternoon while being inspired by their achievements is a remarkable experience for a visitor.

5:30 p.m. The Air Show begins as barnstormers fly over the skies of Atchison.

6:00 p.m. An Invitation is extended to all researchers to attend a delicious buffet at the Amelia Earhart Museum. Another memorable event to enjoy in the company of new and old friends seated on the porch or lawn of the Earhart Birthplace.

At dusk the fireworks over the Missouri River begins. Set to music as the audiences below the skyline are memorized by the rockets of colorful fire shooting across the heavens.

Authors Notation:

While visiting Atchison in 2003, 2004, and 2005, I used my free time to interview other researchers, relatives of Amelia Earhart, and admirers. On July 21, 2007 at the 11th Annual Amelia Earhart Festival, I presented my documentary *Close To Closure: The Amelia Earhart Mystery* at the Atchison Theater to a full audience. Question and answers followed.

Chapter 24.

McKeesport Heritage Center
McKeesport, Pennsylvania

Knowing Amelia Earhart had crisscrossed the United States during her lecture tours, book promotions, and races, I was interested in contacting the Senator John Heinz Regional History Center located in downtown Pittsburgh to verify what they had in their archive department. Sure enough there was a file containing material. Next I made arrangements to visit the Heinz Center to see what they had gathered in the file. I ventured to their top floor archival desk, placed my request, and within minutes a young intern handed me a folder with the name Amelia Earhart typed on it. Just as she handed the folder to me, a small piece of paper dropped to the floor. She slowly bent down, picked it up, glanced at the paper, then looked across to me stating, "This is the obituary of a pilot who grow up in McKeesport. Her name was Helen Richey and was found dead in her New York City apartment in 1947. It has been as mystery as to what happen!" She then opened the folder to slip the obituary notice back into it. Was that meant to happen at that precise moment? Would I have skimmed through the folder not even noticing the Helen Richey obituary?

Knowing my immense interest in female pilots of the Golden Age of Aviation, I can guarantee you I inquired about any files, folders . . . anything on this pilot Helen Richey. She looked up the name on the computer, turned to me and replied, "No we have nothing." If they didn't have anything, than I must be on to something. Gathering as much information I could on Amelia Earhart's visits to Pittsburgh, I returned the folder and made sure I requested a copy of Helen Richey's obituary. I began my investigations immediately upon returning to my home.

Helen Richey was connected to aviation history in a bigger way than I could imagine. She wasn't a household name so I wanted to see what the McKeesport Heritage Center had in their files about their hometown native. Cynthia Neish was the director of the center back in 2005. There was ample material to review on the subject of aviation in McKeesport and Bettis Field. I had to dig some more to locate material on Helen Richey to add to what the center had available. Next, I contacted the town newspaper. Geraldine (Jerry) Jurann worked in the archive area for decades. She assisted me with just about every newspaper article (original) on Helen Richey's career that appeared in the *Daily News*, dating back to her earliest days of flying prior to receiving her permit in 1930. The last item published was her obituary dated January 7, 1947.

I spending months reading, interviewing individuals that knew the Richey family, gathering photos of Helen throughout her career. I pulled information from everywhere possible and followed up any potential lead. I was beginning to become overwhelmed. Why weren't more books written about her accomplishments? The only one on record was *Propeller Annie*, based upon a series of newspaper articles assembled by Glenn Kerfoot (a one time resident of McKeesport) in 1988. What was needed was a documentary. Taking the project even one step further, a docudrama would really illustrate her life on a personal level. That way Helen Richey story could come alive on the big screen.

Thinking I had a good idea, the next step was to make contact with the Heritage Center to discuss the project with their Board of Directors. The project's decision was in the hands of Marilyn Baldwin, Aty. J. Terrence Farrell, Robert Hauser, William Hunter, Duane Junker, Irv Latterman, Daniel Piesik, Robert Messner, Ruth Richards, Jo Anne Rogers, Frances Show, Sue Ann Stiffler, and DeWayne Wivagg. I kept my fingers crossed they would consider my proposal at the next board meeting.

Finally I received the green light to begin the developmental stage of the docudrama. DeWayne Wivagg and his wife Evette were the strongest supports of the idea. Evette, a aviation buff, expressed a firm belief that every young person who lives in McKeesport should knew they had a hero amongst them. I couldn't agree more. Even Amelia Earhart visited the Richey home on Jenny Lind Street. Does it get any better than that? Earhart didn't make too many visits to just anyone's home (other than her own families) in her time. But she made time to visit with the Richeys. The only other pilot Amelia visited was Jackie Cochran in California in the mid to late 1930's.

My goal with the documentary was to give Helen Richey a face. Not just words in a book. So I sought out individuals who knew her personally. I went as far as arranging an interview with her niece, Amy Lannan, who had resided on the island of Hawaii (Hilo) since the early

1980's. After contacting the University of Hawaii's media department, I arranged for a film intern to film an interview at Mrs. Lannan's home. She agreed to assist and the experience was noted on her resume. What a thrill to receive it a week later in my mailbox. The interview covered areas of Helen's career, the first time Amelia Earhart visited the Richey home, Amy's opinion of Jackie Cochran whom she had met on several occasions, Helen living with Amy and her husband in Philadelphia, stories Helen told her while Helen was flying over in England, Ernie Pyle interviewing Helen, and so forth.

Guy P. Gamble (Amy's brother), Betty Shaw-Gamble (Helen's sister-in-law and daughter of the G.C. Murphy Company co-owner), Pearl McCune (a school acquaintance of Helen's), and Donald Riggs (a Pittsburgh television and radio broadcaster) all were included in the interview portion of the documentary. Donald Riggs, with his vast knowledge of Pittsburgh's aviation history, explained how the town of McKeesport, Pennsylvania impacted the air mail service back in the late 1920's. Today every plane that takes off still carries air mail. Helen Richey was part of that generation early in her career.

By the spring of 2005, the docudrama scenes were being planned. I needed the right actress to portray Helen Richey. Helen was five foot, solidly built, brown hair, blue eyes, cheerful, and high energy. Contacting the Apple Hill Playhouse in Delmont, Pennsylvania, the director pointed me to the perfect actress—Elyssa Book, a student majoring in fine arts at Point Park College in Pittsburgh. I met with Elyssa who certainly fit the bill. How lucky I was.

A scene was written with Helen and Frances Marsalis discussing the up-coming 1932 Endurance Race, in which they were to fly over Miami, Florida for at least nine days. Frances had flown with Louise Thaden, in August of 1932 for 196 hours over Valley Stream in New York. Now she wanted to set another record. So Helen and Frances went south to Florida to attempt the feat. They successfully broke the old record, creating a new one of nine days and twenty-one minutes. Kimberly Mallin played a hands-on Francis Marcsalis.

Of course no scene would be complete without the appearance of Amelia Earhart. Kathy Rentz of Johnstown, Pennsylvania who starred in the documentary/docu-drama *Close To Closure*, stepped in to give Helen a pep talk prior to the Endurance Race. I set up the scene with Helen returning the keys to Amelia when she came to McKeesport to pick up her Yellow Pearl car, which Helen had been storing for her while Amelia was flying over to England and France.

One scene, I absolutely had to include was when Jackie Cochran turned over her ATA London command to Helen in 1942, so she could quickly return to the United States to organize the Woman's Air Service Pilots in Sweetwater, Texas. Margaret Ryan, an engineer by day and an actress on weekends, accepted the role as Jackie Cochran. With a southern accent to boot, she nailed it.

The premiere showing of *The Helen Richey Story**at the McKeesport Heritage Center took place on the fourth annual Founders Day on October 8, 2006. Brian Grundy, the executive producer, several of the actresses, and myself arrived that evening to a full house with an enthusiastic audience eager to view the long-awaited story of their hometown heroine. I will always be grateful for the opportunity the Wivagg Foundation offered me to bring Helen Richey home.

*Note: *The Helen Richey Story* on DVD can be purchased through the McKeesport Heritage Center gift shop.

Chapter 25

100th Birthday Celebration
1909-2009

January 2009 marked the beginning of a year-round celebration highlighting the accomplishments of McKeesport's heroine, Helen Richey. The idea was launched by the President of the Board of Director, Robert Hauser. Mrs. Michelle Wardle the Executive Director, her staff, and volunteers all planed activities for the community to attend. The Helen Richey Exhibit first assembled in 2007 had received additional items and all were placed on display inside a beautiful show case, which was donated by Evette and DeWayne Wivagg. The most recent items received were the Congregational Gold Medal of Honor the Gamble family contributed to the center as well as letters, photos, and other articles of interest.

A large bronze plaque was refurbished at the Helen Richey Memorial Field, located across the road from the McKeesport Heritage Center. The plaque was originally erected by the community on May 11, 1954 to honor her. The plaque features Helen dressed in her British Air Transport Auxiliary uniform during World War II. The plaque is engraved with the words:

Born	(Her Picture)	Died
November 21, 1909		January 7, 1947
McKeesport, PA.		New York City

HELEN RICHEY
MEMORIAL FIELD

ONE OF THE FIRST WOMEN FLYERS IN THE
UNITED STATES. SOLOED EARLY IN 1930.
MEMBER OF THE FAMED NINETY NINES NATIONAL
CLUB OF WOMEN FLYERS.

AS A TEEN AGE SCHOOL GIRL SHE BLAZED
A TRAIL TO STARDOM IN STUNT AND COMMERCIAL
FLYING. CLIMAXED BY A BRILLIANT RECORD IN
BRITISH

SHE ESTABLISHED EARLY WORLD ENDURANCE
AND ALTITUDE RECORDS FOR LIGHT PLANES
SURPASSING THE MARK HELD BY MALE FLYERS
AT THE TIME.

IN 1936, FLYING ALONE, SHE CLIMBED TO
18,000 FEET. BREAKING THE EXISTING WORLDS
ALTITUDE RECORD FOR LIGHT PLANES.

McKEESPORT IS PROUD OF HER RECORD.

A proclamation was performed by the McKeesport Mayor James Brewster, read a proclamation as he presented the key to the city to Helen Richey in front of her plaque. The key can be viewed inside the display case at the Heritage Center.

On the warm Sunday afternoon an air show was performed by builders of miniature airplanes. One by one, planes took off into the air as the crowd below applauded with delight. A little reminder of the barnstorming days during Helen's early days as she and other daredevil pilots (in real airplanes) flew over the skies of McKeesport and other towns that made up the Mon-Valley.

On November 21, 2009, at the McKeesport-Versailles Cemetery, a gravesite Commemoration Ceremony was performed. Poems were read by admirers of Helen Richey followed by a 21-gun salute. The closing was conducted by Michelle Wardle, Director of the McKeesport Heritage Center.

Back at the Heritage Center, a red ribbon was cut at the entrance of the main exhibition room with the assistance of Mayor Brewster, DeWayne and Evette Wivagg, Nadine Kerfoot, and Michelle Wardle. This was follow by a delicious catered sit-down dinner for over a hundred guests. Of course, what would a birthday party be without a cake decorated with flowers of the fall season.

The month of December rounded out the year-long celebration with a Christmas Tree decorated with an aviation theme and small photos of Helen Richey. It was a success . . . as was her short life. Rich in courage, silent in sorrow.

Author's Final Thoughts

Helen Richey and Amelia Earhart were linked together far before this book was written. Out of all the female pilots of the "Golden Age of Aviation," they were the greatest. No one took more risks than Amelia and Helen every time they strapped themselves into the seat of a biplane. Amelia herself said that Helen was the best pilot in the world.

When war clouds were brewing in the Far East and Europe, the world lost the innocence it once had. Change was in the forecast. Citizens of the world were asked to make life-altering decisions. Those who answered the call were truly brave at heart.

After a stellar career in the ATA's, serving in England, Helen was needed back in the United States. Again coming to the aid of her country, she enlisted in the WASP organization. Helen had more hours log in the air than any one of the members of the WASP organization including those assigned to Command. Unfortunately, she was made to go through flight training alongside of a bunch of "want-a-be" pilots. That had to be degrading, but the organizer—Jackie Cochran—wasn't satisfied unless she was humiliating Helen. In spite of this, Helen's pride and duty to the United States were unconditional, even through her darkest days.

As the war came to an end in 1945, a new beginning was in sight for Helen. She began a new job and was negotiating the publication of an autobiography, covering her stellar career in aviation. Even with everything going her way, Helen was preoccupied with the disappearance of her friend, Amelia Earhart. Amelia, too, had every-thing going for herself as she topped off her aviation career with the world flight. Then, at the high point of career and fame, she met an undetermined fate. Sound familiar?

Was Helen Richey a victim of fate the evening of January 7, 1947 or was she a victim of who she knew and what she knew?

Photo Gallery

Helen Richey, born Nov. 21, 1909,
in McKeesport, PA to Dr. Joseph
and Amy Richey.
Courtesy of Amy Gamble-Lannan.

Helen and Mrs. Amy Richey
in front of family home on
Jenny Lind Street. *Courtesy of
Amy Gamble-Lannan.*

Helen's first dental appointment.
Courtesy of Amy Gamble-Lannan.

14 year old Helen riding
neighbor's horse.
Courtesy of Amy Gamble-Lannan.

Helen with her brothers and
Gamble cousins. *Courtesy
of Amy   Gamble-Lannan.*

Cleveland Airport, National Air Race
1932. *Courtesy of Dwight D.
Eisenhower Presidential Museum.*

1927 graduation picture of
Helen Richey. *Courtesy of
Amy Gamble-Lannan.*

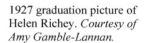

Air Marketing Group on East Coast.
Courtesy of McKeesport Daily News

Helen Richey at Bettis Air field, McKeesport, PA. 1931
Courtesy of Amy Gamble-Lannan.

Instructor at M.I.T., Mass.   Endurance Race, Miami, Fl. 1933.
Helen and male pilot. 1940.   *Courtesy of International Women's*
Courtesy of Amy Gamble-   *Air and Space Museum.*
Lannan

With Miss Ya-Ching Lee,
"China's Amelia Earhat"
Pittsburgh, PA visit 1939.
*Courtes of The Pittsburgh
Press.*

Spectators Theresa James, Miss Lee,
Helen Richey, and Louise Thaden.
Pittsburgh, PA visit 1939.
Courtesy of the Pittsburgh Press.

Amelia Earhart visits
Wilkinsburg on lecture
tour (Helen Richey fourth
from left). *Courtesy of
Wilkinsburg Historical
Society.*

Amelia Earhart and Helen Richey on a visit to Pittsburgh, PA 1932
Courtesy of Amy Gamble-Lannan

Amelia Earhart and Helen Richey on a visit to McKeesport, Pa. 1934 *Courtesy of Amy Gamble-Lannan.*

Central AirLines Amelia Earhart and Helen Richey, Washington, D.C. 1936. *Courtesy of Amy Gamble-Lannan*

Preparing for the Bendix Race, September 1936. *Courtesy of Amy Gamble-Lannan*

Bobby Myers at 15 years of age at Farm Bay Island, CA 1937. *Courtesy of Barbara Wiley.*

Amelia Earhart and Purdue University President Dr. Edward C. Elliott *Courtesy of Perdue University.*

Helen Richey and actor Dick Powell. 1939 Hollywood, California.
Courtesy of Amy Gamble-Lannan

Hawaii 1938
Engagement gathering:
Mr. Soles, Helen,
Jack, Mrs. Soles.
*Courtesy of Amy
Gamble-Lannan.*

Hawaii 1938.
Soles family. *Courtesy
of Amy Gamble-Lannan*

Amelia Earhart (top center) and Fred Noonan (black shirt) at
Venezuelan airport, Lae, New Guinea. This is their last public photo
together. July 2, 1937. *Courtesy of Henry Beville.*

Jackie Cochran and Helen Richey
(1942) aboard a Hurricane
aircraft. *Courtesy of Keystone
Press, London.*

Helen Richey in Britain's Air
Transport Auxiliary uniform.
Courtesy of Amy Gamble-Lannan.

Mrs. Roosevelt and American female ATA pilots.
Courtesy of Keystone Press, London.

American pilots of the ATA's. Helen (3rd from left), Pauline Gower,
Commander of the ATA's (standing on the right).
Courtesy of Keystone Press, London.

Sweet Water, Texas. Avenger Field WASP's last dinner together.
Helen (front row, kneeling, second from the left).
Courtesy of Texas Women's University.

Theresa James and Helen Richey stationed at New Castle, Delaware.
Courtesy of Wilkinsburg Historical Society.

Helen Richey and Esther Nelson at Fairfax field, Kansas City, Kansas.

Courtesy of Dwight D. Eisenhower Presidential Museum, Helen Richey collection.

Helen Richey in the U.S. Women's Airforce Service Pilot uniform. *Courtesy of Amy Gamble-Lannan.*

Leo Bellarts. Radio man on ITASCA, July 1937. *Courtesy of David Bellarts.*

Thomas Devine, active duty on Saipan 1945. *Courtesy of Ann Devine.*

Fred Goerner 1966 book signing at KCBS San Francisco, CA.
Courtesy of Lily Gelb.

Joe Gervais at his home, March 2003. *Courtesy of author.*

Elgen Long book signing "Breakfast with the Authors"
Amelia Earhart Festival, 2003. *Courtesy of author.*

Louise Foudray and Amelia Rose Earhart at the
Amelia Earhart Birthplace Museum.
Courtesy of Louise Foudray.

November 2009: Helen Richey's 100 Birthday Celebration
at the McKeesport Heritage Center.

McKeesport Heritage Center Director, Michelle Wardle.

McKeesport Cemetery
grave site with WASP
marker.

Appendix

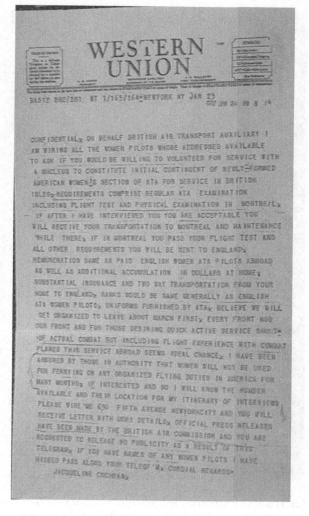

Western Union telegram from Jackie Cochran to Helen Richey (1942). *Dwight D. Eisenhower Presidential Museum, Helen Richey Collection.*

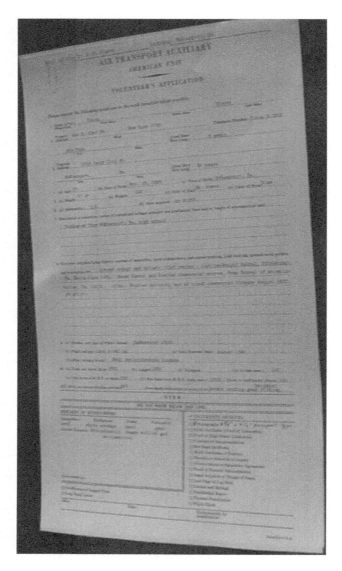

Air Transport Auxiliary application. *Dwight D. Eisenhower*
Presidential Museum, Helen Richey Collection

Appendix

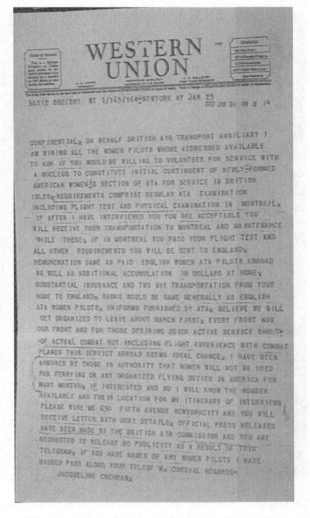

Western Union telegram from Jackie Cochran to Helen Richey (1942).
Dwight D. Eisenhower Presidential Museum, Helen Richey Collection.

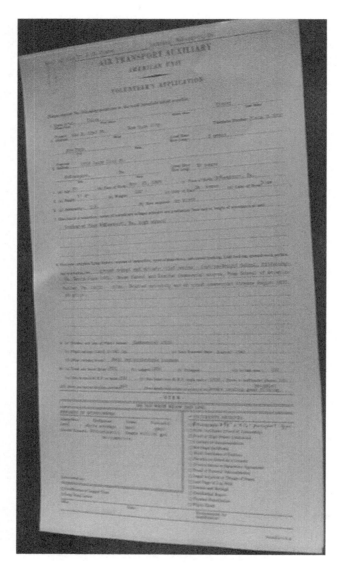

Air Transport Auxiliary application. *Dwight D. Eisenhower Presidential Museum, Helen Richey Collection*

Air Transport Auxiliary card of Helen Richey.
Amy Gamble-Lannan.

Air Transport Handbook of Helen Richey.
Maidenhead Heritage Center.

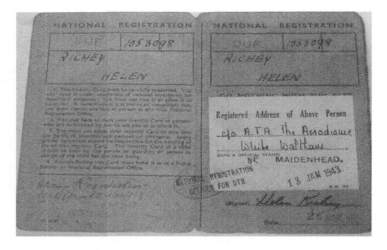

National Registration Maidenhead, England.
Maidenhead Heritage Center.

Air Transport Auxiliary Plane Transport Slip.
Maidenhead Heritage Center.

Letter from Ernie Pyle (December 4, 1944)
The Lilly Library, University of Indiana
Ernie Pyle Collection/Helen Richey

Article (October 15, 1942) by Ernie Pyle.
The Lilly Library, University of Indiana
Ernie Pyle Collection/Helen Richey.

Pan American Airways-Africa, Limited
Page 1 of Helen Richey's application (1942)

Pan American Airways-Africa, Limited
Page 2 of Helen Richey's application (1943)

Helen Richey's WASP Certification # 15151
Dwight D. Eisenhower Presidential Museum

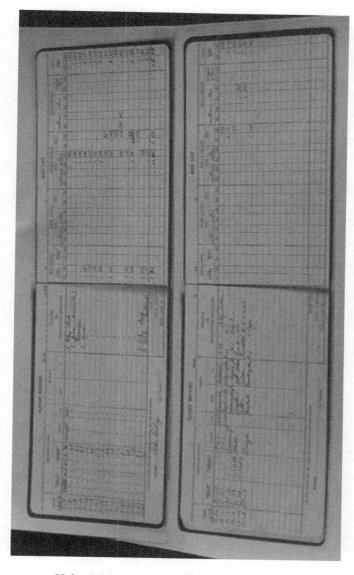

Helen Richey's WASP Certification # 15151
Smithsonian Air and Space Museum

Autopsy on Flyer (January 8, 1947)
Associated Press

January 12 1965

Mrs. Muriel Earhart Morrissey
1 Vernon St.
West Medford, Mass.

My Dear Mrs. Morrissey:

I have respected your wishes over the years concerning your thoughts relating to the fate of Amelia. Naturally, you are unaware of all that has transpired since my visit with you in the summer of 1961.

After much difficulty I arrived on Saipan in December, 1963 where a preliminary survey enabled me to pin-point the area where in 1945 a native woman disclosed a hidden grave-site area which contained the remains of a white man and a white woman who had come from the sky. This fact and my eye-witness information concerning their plane at Aslito Field in 1944 and the disposition thereof has prompted me to assemble much additional information.

It is my intention to return to Saipan to excavate the site.

There are many technicalities; and of course prior approval of next of kin is necessary to transport the remains from the Trust Territory. It has been suggested by an official of the Interior Dept., that I secure a written statement to this effect.

I respectfully request your approval at your earliest possible convenience.

Sincerely,

Thomas E. Devine
8? Isadore St.
West Haven 16 Conn. 06516

Letter from Thomas Devine (January 12, 1965)

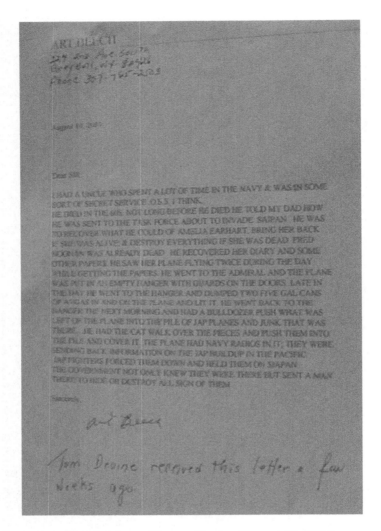

Art Beech letter to Thomas Devine (August 10, 2003)

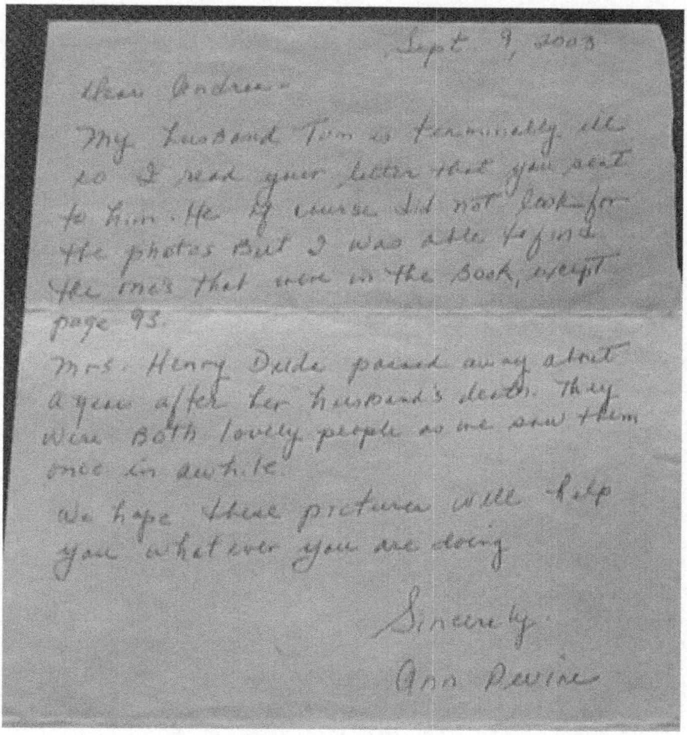

Sept. 9, 2003

Dear Andrew-

My husband Tom is terminally ill so I read your letter that you sent to him. He of course did not look for the photos But I was able to find the ones that were in the Book, except page 93.

Mrs. Henry Deide passed away about a year after her husband's death. They were Both lovely people so we saw them once in awhile.

We hope these pictures will help you what ever you are doing

Sincerely
Ann Devine

Mrs. Ann Devine's letter to author (September 9, 2003

Today's News Today
Latest Markets

ATCHISON

PRICE FIVE CENTS.   ATCHISON, KANSAS, S

Central Branch Farmers Will Play Golf This Summer,

AMELIA'S VOICE HEARD BY AMATEUR RADIO OPERATOR

Distress Signal Buoys Hoped For Ultimate Rescue of Aviatrix

PLANE ADRIFT AT SEA

Former Atchison Girl and Companion Forced Down When Fuel Is Exhausted On Perilous Flight

(By The Associated Press)

Honolulu, July 3—Reports that the voice of tousle-haired Amelia Earhart had been picked up, calling "SOS" from the mystery spot where she is lost in mid-Pacific, buoyed hopes for her ultimate rescue today as the U. S. navy ordered a battleship into the search.

Two Los Angeles amateur radio operators as late as 7 a. m. Pacific Time (9 a. m. C. S. T.) said they distinctly heard her sound her call letters, KHAQQ, after thrice saying "SO" some 20 minutes earlier.

At San Francisco, however, a coast guard station reported at noon Eastern Standard time it had received no word whatever although radio reception was unusually good.

Earlier the Los Angeles operators Walter McMenamy and Carl Pierson interpreted radio signals as placing the plane adrift near the equator between Gilbert islands and Howland island, the latter Miss Earhart's destination, when her fuel was exhausted more than 20 hours before.

At Washington, the navy department ordered the battleship Colorado with three planes aboard to begin a search from Honolulu, where it arrived yesterday.

Throughout the night, the Itasca stationed at Howland originally to assist the aviatrix and Noonan, scoured the waters within a 100 miles radius of the island, watching for distress flares.

In the glare of the rising sun, officers of the Itasca said, Miss Earhart apparently overshot the island, a mere sand spit a mile and a half long and but two feet above the water, and was forced down, a short time later.

Exactly where she alighted, no one could say, and just how long the twin-motored ship could stay afloat was a disputed point. One of her last messages indicated the plane was within 100 miles of Howland island.

At Los Angeles, Mrs. E. B. Earhart, her stepmother, said resolutely: "I am sure Amelia will come through."

"Amelia believes in preparedness," she said. "If she is in trouble—and somehow I feel she is not—she'll find her way out. I know that she carried a collapsible rubber boat for use in case of a forced landing."

Putnam Confident

Paul Mantz, technical adviser to the aviatrix, who twice crossed the Atlantic, said in Burbank, Calif., the plane's six gas tanks would give it buoyancy to stay afloat "indefinitely."

George Palmer Putnam, husband of the missing flier, was in constant communication with coast guard headquarters at San Francisco. He expressed belief his wife and her companion would be found safe.

"The plane should float, but I couldn't estimate how long because a Lockheed plane has never been forced down at sea before."

The plane had a two man rubber lifeboat, life belts, flares, a signal kite and emergency food and water rations.

The Itasca began its search as soon as officers determined the ship must have been forced down.

The minesweep Swan was ordered south from its position last night, but was not expected to reach the Howland island area for some time.

Headwinds and static combined to plague the fliers almost from the time they left Lae They were unable to communicate with the Itasca because of the static and the adverse winds cut speed and increased fuel consumption.

C. I. O. PURGE IS UNDER WAY

Gus Hall and Others "Canned" In Cleanup

COMMUNISTS IN STRIKE

Claim Party and Members Participated in Drive to Organize Steel

(By The Associated Press)

Youngstown, O., July 3—A CIO "purge" began today, as the union's axe fell on Gus Hall and two other strike captains in the Mahoning valley steel sector.

John Owens, general C. I. O. strike director in Ohio, announced without comment the removal of Hall, now in jail under charges of heading a "dynamite ring," as strike captain in the Warren area. A joint leadership of Harry Winns and John Grazier replaced him.

Owens also stripped two of his Youngstown strike lieutenants of their authority, removing Ben Butler, chief organizer at the Republic Steel plant, and John Stevenson, organizer at the main plant of the Youngstown Sheet & Tube Co.

Communist participation in the strike was claimed in circulars distributed through the valley today. In the circulars Phil Bart, "Mahoning valley secretary of the Communist party," said:

"Of course, the Communist party and its members in the steel town participated in the drive to organize steel and all other unorganized industries. The Communist party joins with all democratic forces in the struggle against reactionaries, open shop violence, and fascism."

Owens' "housecleaning" order was issued only a few hours after another prominent chieftain of the C. I. O. movement—Homer Martin, head of the automobile workers—removed three union organizers at Flint, Mich., and transferred a Detroit organizer from his post. The action, he explained, was "disciplinary" and followed several unauthorized strikes at General Motors plants.

Governor Frank Murphy deplored Communist activities which, at Law-

Front page of the *Atchison Daily Globe*, Atchison, Kansas, July 3, 1937

HEAR AMELIA'S VOICE

(Continued from page 1)

recently flew here from California, and from San Diego to Panama, would be able to cover thousands of square miles in a comparatively short while.

Howland Island is a treeless sandspot located strategically on a direct air line from Honolulu to Australia. Hawaiian school boys have been maintained on the island by the United States government to make weather observations. Plans have been made to lay out a permanent airfield.

MAY HAVE LANDED ON SMALL ISLAND NEAR DESTINATION

(By The Associated Press)

Oakland, Calif., July 3. — A theory that Amelia Earhart might have brought her plane down safely on a small coral atoll south of Howland was advanced today by her technical adviser, Paul Mantz, in a telephone conversation with George Palmer Putnam.

Putnam, husband of the aviatrix, said he conferred with Mantz at Burbank.

Mantz said he believed she landed on one of the Phoenix islands, a group southeast of the Howland island.

"Several of the Phoenix islands are large enough to allow a plane to land," Mantz was quoted by Putnam. "The undercarriage might have been damaged but the fliers could have walked away from the plane uninjured."

Mantz expressed the belief the plane's main battery or generator, and the emergency set for the radio probably were put out of commission if the plane came down on the ocean.

He said the main battery was under the fuselage and the emergency one was inside. The emergency battery might have been protected from the water, Mantz said, but added that he doubted this.

He explained the main radio equipment was under the pilot's seat in the cockpit and could have escaped damage.

Because both Miss Earhart and her navigator, Fred Noonan, were experienced and cool in the face of danger, Mantz said he believed they had "sat" the plane down under its own power when Miss Earhart realized the emergency.

Should they have alighted safely on an atoll, Mantz said he thought it possible they had rigged up the radio to broadcast word of their plight.

He stated the radio was both a code and voice apparatus, but that Miss Earhart probably would speak into it because she and Noonan were only novices at code.

Continued from the front page of the
Atchison Daily Globe, July 3, 1937

SHIPS OF THREE NATIONS SPUR SEARCH FOR AMELIA

Meteors Mistaken For Flares As Vessels Widen Hunt For Lost Plane

MYSTERY IN MESSAGES

Conflicting Radio Reports Still Being Received—Belief Earhart and Navigator on Remote Coral Reef Strengthened

(By The Associated Press)

Honolulu, July 6—Vessels from three nations pursued the widening mid-Pacific search today for Amelia Earhart, after a meteor was mistaken for flares from her missing plane.

The long-searching coast guard cutter Itasca, which encountered the lights that proved to be meteors, advised Washington at 11:54 a. m. (C. S. T.) no new information was available on the missing first lady of the air.

Another radio amateur at Oakland, Calif., reported he picked up a message from the aviatrix at 8:30 a. m. (C. S. T.) despite that authorities agreed she could not broadcast had her plane alighted on the water and further that the approximate position indicated already had been searched unsuccessfully by the cutter Itasca.

The amateur, Charles Miguel, said the message read: "281 north Howland. Cannot hold out much longer. Drifting southwest. We above water. Motor sinking in water. Very wet."

Coast guard officials at San Francisco and George Palmer Putnam, husband of Miss Earhart, began an investigation of Miguel's report, which was ...

The Weather

Kansas—Generally fair tonight and Wednesday; not so warm in northwest portion Wednesday.

Missouri—Partly cloudy, tonight and Wednesday; somewhat warmer in east and south Wednesday.

Nebraska—Partly cloudy and somewhat unsettled tonight and Wednesday, possibly local thundershowers in extreme east Wednesday; somewhat cooler Wednesday and in northwest tonight.

Thermometer Readings

8 a. m.	84	Noon	95
9 a. m.	89	1 p. m.	98
10 a. m.	92	2 p. m.	99
11 a. m.	94	3 p. m.	100

Lowest last night 70. Temperature here a year ago this afternoon 101.

Weather and Dirt Roads

(By The Associated Press)

Manhattan, Coffeyville, Ottawa, Emporia—Clear; roads good.

Pittsburg—Clear; roads good.

Arkansas City, Wichita—Clear; roads good.

Salina—Clear; roads good.

Topeka—Clear; roads good.

ANOTHER BODY FOUND IN SERIES OF TORSO MURDERS

(By The Associated Press)

Cleveland, July 6—The headless body of a man, described by Chief Detective Inspector Joseph Sweeney as Cleveland's tenth torso murder victim, was taken from the Cuyahoga river near a railroad bridge here today.

Inspector Sweeney said the torso was discovered by two national guardsmen, in Cleveland for steel strike duty.

The detective-inspector said that the head of the victim had been severed cleanly as in all of the previous killings.

The skeleton of the ninth victim of the head hunter, a Negro woman about 35 years old, was found less than a month ago under a Cuyahoga river bridge not far from the spot where the torso was found today.

Today's victim was the sixth man to fall before the killer's knife. Four women have been decapitated and dismembered in the series of killings.

Front page of the *Atchinson Daily Globe*, July 5, 1937

NO TRACE OF AMELIA

(Continued from page 1)

Phoenix islands, but had more than 500 miles to go.

Beginning at Winslow reef, some 175 miles east of Howland and continuing south, to the northern edge of the Phoenix group, charts show the presence of reefs and islets which might offer haven to a plane.

About 180 miles southeast of Howland lies a charted sandspit which officials said might offer an emergency landing spot.

The Colorado, veering from the area north of Howland, was to proceed toward the Winslow bank region after contacting the Itasca.

Putnam again took up vigil in the San Francisco coast guard radio headquarters last night. He appeared cheerful.

Paul Mantz, technical adviser to Miss Earhart, reiterated belief the plane could float "indefinitely."

Mrs. Beatrice Noonan, the missing navigator's wife, who collapsed Sunday, was sufficiently recovered yesterday to return to the beauty shop she operates.

Rubber Boat Is Her Last Resort

If storms battered apart the floating plane, Amelia Earhart could still "take to the boat." A collapsible rubber lifeboat, big enough to hold two persons, was part of the equipment of her "Flying Laboratory." Miss Earhart (above) inflates it with a hand pump, in a test before the start of her flight.

Cutter Searches for Amelia

The 250-foot coast guard cutter Itasca (above), stationed at Howland Island, steamed the Southern Pacific in a hunt for Amelia Earhart whose plane apparently was down at sea. America's leading woman flier had expected to stop at Howland Island and fliers feared she overshot the small sandspit and had insufficient fuel to return.

All images contnued from front page of *Atchinson Daily Globe*, July 5, 1937

STILL NO TRACE OF LOST FLIERS

Search For Amelia Shifts to New Region

PLANES INTO HUNT TODAY

Colorado Expected to Launch Airplanes in Vicinity of Howland Island

Putnam to Honolulu

San Francisco, July 7.—A tentative reservation on the Philippine Clipper plane, leaving at 3 p. m. (P. S. T.) today for Honolulu was made by George Palmer Putnam, husband of the missing flier, Amelia Earhart. Pan American officials informed Putnam that a seat in the plane was available.

(By The Associated Press)

Honolulu, July 7.— Navy ships and planes, coordinating efforts in the vast hunt for Amelia Earhart, aimed today at a new region in the South Pacific wastes where growing belief and some facts indicated the missing aviatrix may be marooned.

The coast guard at San Francisco said it had been checking with the cutter Itasca throughout the day but had no news of the missing aviatrix and her navigator.

Walter McMenamy and Carl Pierson, Los Angeles amateur operators who have eight receiving sets operating, said they had heard nothing on the Earhart wave length throughout the night and doubted if other amateurs had picked up anything because all operators have been requested to notify them of any reception.

Five discouraging days of scanning the immense area north northeast of bleak Howland island, which the aviatrix missed last Friday, turned the search to the corresponding area centered south southeast of Howland, where 280 miles away center the Phoenix islands.

The coast guard cutter Itasca and

Front page story from the *Atchinson Daily Globe*, July 6, 1937

Continuation of front page story in the *Atchinson Daily Globe*,
July 6, 1937

Continuation of front page story in the *Atchinson Daily Globe*, July 6, 1937

When Amelia Joked About Howland Island

Several months ago, when Amelia Earhart disclosed plans for her round-the-world flight, a reporter asked how big Howland Island looked on the map compared to other places she would visit and she smilingly held up her hand as shown. She apparently overshot the island, however, on her flight from New Guinea and is the object of a far-flung search in the Southern Pacific.

Atchinson Daily Globe, July 6, 1937

VAST HUNT FOR MISSING FLIERS

Navy Launches Mightiest Peacetime Search in History

NEW MESSAGE SOARS HOPES

Amateur Radio Operator Picks Up Man's Voice — A Position Given

(By The Associated Press)

Honolulu, July 8 — The mightiest peacetime search of the United States navy was launched today for Amelia Earhart, missing round-the-world flier, who officials hope is awaiting rescue on a coral reef or sandpit somewhere southeast of tiny Howland island.

The battleship Colorado, cruising south and east of Howland, catapulted its three fighting planes last night to open the aerial phase of the hunt undertaken by boat when Miss Earhart failed to arrive at Howland last Friday on a 2,570-mile flight from New Guinea.

The Colorado's aircraft returned to the battleship after two hours and 20 minutes to report no trace had been sighted of the missing plane or of Miss Earhart and her navigator, Fred Noonan.

The planes planned to resume their search today at dawn, (11:30 a. m. Central Standard Time), cruising over Winslow reef, 120 miles below the equator and southeast of Howland Island.

From the vicinity of Winslow reef the Colorado could catapult her planes into a search of many islets and reefs in the northern Phoenix islands.

Within flying distance to the southeast would be Canton island, site of

Could Live A Month

(By The Associated Press)

San Francisco, July 8—Amelia Earhart and Fred Noonan apparently could live for a month or more if they landed on an equatorial islet as searchers believed today.

They were the only ones who

Front page article in the *Atchinson Daily Globe*, July 8, 1937

Continuation of the front page story in the
Atchinson Daily Globe, july 8, 1937

William Allen White. writing about Amelia Earhart: "Sooner or later it had to come. Her luck was a curve that would end in tragedy. It is curious about luck. Some people go through life breaking arms, legs, having queer, unaccountable illnesses, mishaps, disasters, calamities following in their trains; others lead smooth, unbroken lives. Something in character determines destiny. It is too mysterious to be put down in anything like mathematical certainty. But the hunches of men—meaning by which, intuitions—tell us something about destiny in everything, in particular everything connected with man's fate. Some way a man's character makes his destiny, some way physical equipment, the capacity for exact, co-ordination between eyes, hand, feet, the muscular reactions of the body, affect character. Destiny, of course, has a physical basis in the qualities of man. Poor Amelia had been biffed, banged, battered about in her career as a flyer. How inevitable it was that she should end in catastrophe. But she has been a great spirit, has added her mite to the wisdom, amusement, happiness of her day and time."

Continuation of the front page article in the
Atchinson Daily Globe, July 8, 1937

AMELIA'S FATE STILL MYSTERY

Aerial Search For Lost Fliers Continues, However

LEXINGTON SPEEDS TO SCENE

Still Report Radio Messages— Belief Grows They Will Never Be Found

(By The Associated Press)

Honolulu, July 9 — Navy aviators, empty handed after two days of search for Amelia Earhart, charted courses across new sections of the equatorial Pacific today in efforts to pierce the week-long mystery of her fate.

By sea and air search for the missing aviatrix and her navigator, Frederick J. Noonan, has encompassed approximately 136,000 square miles without even sighting some of the shoals and sand spits supposed to exist in the vast area.

The flyers vanished a week ago today in an attempt to fly the 2,750-miles from Lae, New Guinea, to Howland Island, a dot of land but two feet above the sea.

Three planes from the battleship Colorado, steaming steadily from the equator southward to the Phoenix islands, soared over the area east and south of Howland islands yesterday but sighted no trace of the pair.

The planes, piloted by Lieuts. J. O. Lambrecht, L. O. Fox, and W. B.

Front page article in the *Atchinson Daily Globe*, July 9, 1037

Colorado, steaming steadily from the equator southward to the Phoenix islands, soared over the area east and south of Howland islands yesterday but sighted no trace of the pair.

The plane, piloted by Lieut. J. O. Lambrecht, L. O. Fox, and W. B. Short, Jr., could not even find Winslow reef, which old charts showed poised just above the sea 175 miles southeast of Howland.

Mariners expressed belief the only available charts either misrepresented the location of the reef, which might have offered a precarious emergency landing spot, or else the little known out-cropping had sunk below the sea's surface.

The Colorado's fliers, awaiting aid over the week-end from the aircraft carrier Lexington's plan, Admiral, today planned to swing southward once again but came back on a course west of the Phoenix and Howland islands.

This expedition would cover area previously unexplored by the coast guard cutter Itasca, which carried on the search alone for days near Howland islands before the Colorado sped southward from Hawaii, more than 1,500 miles away.

Yesterday's flight of more than 500 miles after the planes were catapulted from the battleship's deck covered hundreds of square miles not previously scanned.

Today the aviators planned to go as far south as Gardner island and Carondelet reef, the southernmost part of the Phoenix islands, which render 250 miles south of lonely Howland.

Planes from the Colorado, which was proceeding cautiously to avoid uncharted reefs in the little traversed equatorial area, were expected to complete search of the Phoenix group before arrival of the Lexington, being refueled at Lahaina Roads, near Honolulu.

The $40,000,000 aircraft carrier, which sped from San Diego to Hawaii, was expected to get away for the 1,300-mile dash to the search area today and spread her brood of planes probably next Monday.

Last reported in the vicinity of Baker island, 40 miles south of Howland, the Itasca planned to continue search southward to the Phoenix group, aided by the mine sweeper Swan.

Should today's search prove fruitless the naval fliers planned to spend Saturday combing the northeast portions of the Phoenix group, including Canton island, largest of the chain.

Rear Admiral O. G. Murfin, 14th naval district commandant and director of the search, expressed belief the success or failure of the hunt should be known by Monday, after the Lexington's planes, capable of covering 60,000 square miles daily, begin explorations.

Radio amateurs in Hawaii and on the mainland continued to report interception of messages they interpreted as being from Miss Earhart, but coast guard and naval observers said they had not heard them, and in most instances pointed out the reported calls were on frequencies not used by the aviatrix.

David Binney Putnam, Miss Earhart's stepson, yesterday joined his father, George Palmer Putnam, in San Francisco radiating a confidence not shared in opinions privately expressed by air men and radio operators who have closely followed the search.

steadily today as the sun-baked northern tier of states looked in vain for relief.

At least 56 persons succumbed to the merciless temperatures that extended from the Atlantic coast to eastern Washington. There were hundreds of prostrations. Death by drowning claimed scores of persons among the tens of thousands who sought relief at beaches.

The stifling heat, hitherto confined to the region east of the Rockies, pushed toward the Pacific coast. Redding, Calif. and Yuma, Ariz., each with 104 degrees, were the hottest spots in the United States yesterday. Walla Walla, Wash. sweltered in 96 degree weather yesterday, and Yakima, Wash., recorded 94. Lamar, Colo., and Atlantic, Ia., with readings of 102, were the hottest spots east of the Rockies.

Little change in temperature was in sight outside of New York and New England where slightly cooler weather was forecast.

Fifteen deaths in Michigan were attributed to the heat. Massachusetts reported 11, Connecticut eight; Illinois, seven; Minnesota, Nebraska and New York, three each; Rhode Island, two; Maine, Indiana, West Virginia, Iowa and Ohio, one each.

Temperatures in the upper nineties were general in the middlewestern farm belt and in numerous eastern cities.

In New York City, whose normal average for July is 73 degrees, thermometers yesterday registered maximums of 94 to 98, the city's hottest day this year. Boston reported 99 degrees, the highest July 8 mark in weather bureau records there.

Albany, N. Y., Dodge City, Kas. and Rapid City, S. D. reported readings of 98 degrees; Wichita, Kas., Detroit, La Crosse, Wis. Davenport, Sioux City and Dubuque, Ia., and Omaha, Neb. 96; Milwaukee, Des Moines, Kansas City, Philadelphia, Pittsburgh and Washington, 94.

Chicago suffered from excessive humidity. The maximum temperature was 89 but lack of a lake breeze left the city limpid.

Leadville, Colo., high in the Rockies, was chilled with a night temperature of 38.

CROP ESTIMATES

(By The Associated Press)

Washington, July 9—The agriculture department said today a 3,571,851,000 bushel corn crop and a 882,277,000 bushel wheat crop were indicated by July 1 conditions.

Farms produced 1,509,327 bushels of corn last year, while the five-year (1928-32) average production was 2,504,772,000 bushels.

The total indicated wheat crop, combining winter and spring, compared with $626,461,000 bushels last year and an 864,532,000 bushel five-year average.

Department forecasters estimated winter wheat production at 563,647,000 bushels, compared with 648,597,000 indicated a month ago, 512,013,000 produced last year, and 625,276, the five-year average.

They said the indicated production of all spring wheat was 318,630,000 bushels, compared with 107,443,000 bushels last year and 241,815,000, the five-year average.

Durum wheat production was estimated at 39,366,000 bushels, compared with 8,179,000 last year, and 53,681,000, the five-year average.

Continuation of the front page article in the *Atchinson Daily Globe*, July 9, 1937 the aviatrix.

David Binney Putnam, Miss Earhart's stepson, yesterday joined his father, George Palmer Putnam, in San Francisco radiating a confidence not shared in opinions privately expressed by air men and radio operators who have closely followed the search.

As the extent of the hunt widened, the belief has steadily grown that Miss Earhart and Noonan never would be found.

Continuation of the front page article in the *Atchinson Daily Globe*, July 9, 1937

A week ago today came the news that Amelia Earhart was lost on the Pacific ocean. The Globe regrets to state that the news today about Amelia is not encouraging. By the way, some people are deploring the expense of the search for Amelia. They should remember that manuevers by the navy cost as much as the search for the missing aviatrix. And another thing: If one of your relatives were lost anywhere, you would yell your head off for government assistance.

Amelia and Noonan at Caripito

This picture of Amelia Earhart and Fred Noonan (right) with an unidentified South American, taken in Caripito, Venezuela, was received by the missing woman's husband, George Palmer Putnam at Oakland, Calif. as navy ships searched the South Pacific for the lost fliers.

Atchinson Daily Globe, July 9, 1937

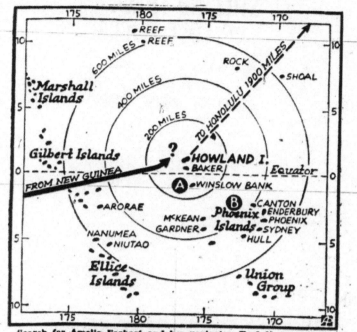

Earhart Search Centers in Islands

Search for Amelia Earhart and her navigator, Fred Noonan, was concentrated in the reefs and islands between Winslow bank (a) and the Phoenix islands (b) after the navy took over direction of the farflung hunt. This Associated Press map shows the area being combed by ships and planes.

Atchinson Daily Globe, July 9, 1937

STILL NO TRACE OF LOST FLIERS

Final Stages of Aerial Search This Week-End

CHANCE OF RESCUE FADES

Little Hope Held That Amelia and Noonan Will Be Found

(By The Associated Press)

Honolulu, July /10—Three navy planes were ordered catapulted over the major group of the Phoenix Islands today in a search which naval officers said would probably reveal whether Amelia Earhart is still alive.

The battleship Colorado's searching planes, shooting into the air at 11:20 a. m. Central Standard Time, were directed to sweep over Enderbury, Phoenix, Birnie and Sydney Islands.

Shore patrols from the minesweeper Swan were ordered to comb Canton, largest of the Phoenix Islands, while the planes scout other possible refuges of Miss Earhart and Fred Noonan, navigator of her round-the-world plane, missing eight days.

The two ships set a rendezvous 15 miles south of Canton at 3:30 p. m. Central Standard Time, to refuel the minesweeper. The Colorado's planes may then survey Canton from the air.

If these searchers do not reveal trace of the missing aviators, naval officers said there was scant hope of their being found in the projected search by 63 planes from the aircraft carrier Lexington, now speeding toward tropic waters from Hawaii.

The Colorado steamed north today. The coast guard cutter Itasca continued parallel to the equator in a methodical search southward.

These three vessels and three planes

Front page article from the Atchinson Daily Globe,
July 10, 1937

alive.

The battleship Colorado's searching pilots, shooting into the air at 11:29 a. m. Central Standard Time, were directed to sweep over Enderbury, Phoenix, Birnie and Sydney islands.

Shore patrols from the minesweeper Swan were ordered to comb Canton, largest of the Phoenix islands, while the planes scout other possible refuges of Miss Earhart and Fred Noonan, navigator of her round-the-world plane, missing eight days.

The two ships set a rendezvous 15 miles south of Canton at 3:30 p. m. Central Standard Time, to refuel the minesweeper. The Colorado's planes may then survey Canton from the air.

If these searchers do not reveal trace of the missing aviators, naval officers said there was scant hope of their being found in the projected search by 64 planes from the aircraft carrier Lexington, now speeding toward tropic waters from Hawaii.

The Colorado steamed north today. The coast guard cutter Itasca continued parallel to the equator in a methodical search southward.

These three vessels and three planes already in the search have covered an area estimated at more than 142,000 square miles since the aviatrix vanished near Howland Island July 2 on a flight there from New Guinea.

Yesterday, a plane from the battleship Colorado alighted in a lagoon at Hull Island, southernmost of the Phoenix group, and the crew asked inhabitants if they saw or heard a plane about the time Miss Earhart broadcast her fuel was nearly gone and she could not sight land. A handful of whites and natives could give no help.

Lexington Due Monday

Lieut. J. O. Lambrecht, who piloted the plane, said he got "the impression they do not know who Miss Earhart is."

Some of the 200 natives on the island paddled a British resident out to the plane, Lieutenant Lambrecht said. The white man reported there was a small radio on the island but no one had seen or heard the plane.

The island's inhabitants are much like castaways, gathering guano and copra. They live in grass huts.

Rear Admiral O. G. Murfin, directing the hunt from here, said an area of about 265,000 square miles stretching in every direction from the barren sandspit Miss Earhart missed on her round the world flight would be covered before the search is called off.

The aircraft carrier Lexington, 440,000,000 navy speed queen, ploughed toward the equator from Hawaii, expecting to launch its 62 planes into the search by Monday morning. She made 31 knots on portions of the voyage from California.

Refueled at nearby Lahaina Roads after a dash from SanDiego, the Lexington left here yesterday at 3:25 p. m. (7:55 p. m. Central Standard Time) for the 1,500 mile sprint to Howland.

While naval officials publicly expressed hope the missing pair would be found, many privately conceded their chances of rescue were practically nil.

(Continued on page 7)

Continuation of article in the *Atchinson Daily Globe*,

July 10, 1937

NO TRACE OF FLIERS

(Continued from page 1)

existent, because a minute search of sea and land within hundreds of miles of Howland has netted not a clue. Remaining hopes rested on the Lexington's planes, which can spread fanwise from the big carrier's deck and virtually blanket all areas where Miss Earhart's land plane possibly could have landed when its fuel ran out.

Continuation of article in the *Atchinson Daily Globe*,
July 10, 1937

Bibliography

Bowman, David K. *Legerdemain*. Bloomington: Author House, 2005.

Briand, Paul. *Daughter of the Sky*. New York: Duell, Sloan and Pearce, 1960.

Brink, Randall. *Lost Star: The Search for Amelia Earhart*. New York: W.W. Norton Co., 1993.

Butler, Susan. *East to the Dawn*. Cambridge: Da Capo Press.

Cochran, Jacqueline. *The Stars at Noon*. Boston: Little, Brown, and Co., 1954.

Devine, Thomas, with Richard D. Daley. *Eyewitness: The Amelia Earhart Incident*. Frederick: Renaissance House, 1987.

Devine, Thomas, with Mike Campbell. *With Our Own Eyes: Eyewitnesses to the Final Days of Amelia Earhart*. Lancaster: Lucky Press, 2002.

Earhart, Amelia. *Last Flight*, New York: Harcourt, Brace and Co., 1937.

Earhart, Amelia. *The Fun of It*, Brooklyn: Braunworth and Co., 1932.

Goerner, Fred. *The Search for Amelia Earhart*. New York: Doubleday, 1966.

Goldstein, Donald M. and Katherin V. Dillon. *Amelia: A Life of the Aviation Legend*, Washington: Brassey's, 1997.

Granger, Byrd Howell. *On Final Approach*. Scottsdale: Falconer Publishing Co.

Kerfoot, Glenn. *Propeller Annie*. Lexington: The Kentucky Aviation History Roundtable, 1988.

Klaas, Joe. *Amelia Earhart Lives*. New York: McGraw Hill, 1970

Long, Elgen and Marie. *Amelia Earhart . . . The Mystery Solved*. New York: Simon and Schuster, 1999.

Lovell, Mary S. *The Sound of Wings*. New York: St. Martin's Press, 1989.

Morrissey, Muriel. *Courage is the Price*. Wichita: McCormick-Armstrong Publishing Division, 1963.

Myers, Robert H. *Stand By to Die: The Disappearance, Rescue, and Return of Amelia Earhart*. Grove: Lighthouse Writers' Guild, 1985.

Putnam, G.P. Jr. *Soaring Wings*. New York: Harcourt, Brace and Co., 1939.

Pyle, Ernie. *Here Is Your War*. New York: Henry Holt and Co., 1943.

Reineck, Rollin C. *Amelia Earhart Survived*. California: The Paragon Agency, 2003.

Rickman, Sarah Byrn. *The Originals*. Sarasota: Disc-Us Books, Inc., 2001.

ABOUT THE AUTHOR

ANDREA NIAPAS is an author and documentary filmmaker based in Ligonier, PA. She was a consultant for the Discovery Channel's investigative series "In Cold Blood" and "Deadly Sins," based on her first book, *Death Needs Answers: The Cold-Blooded Murder of Dr. John Yelenic*, which focused on the violent stabbing death of the popular Blairsville, PA dentist by a Pennsylvania State Trooper.

As a documentary filmmaker Andrea has researched and produced several films. including *The Helen Richey Story* and *Close to Closure*, a documentary about Amelia Earhart.

Recognizing that the death of an individual causes a ripple effect of pain and suffering among family members, friends, and community, she has become a victim's advocate, dedicating much of her time and resources to helping and giving a voice to the co-victims of homicides.

DAVID K. BOWMAN is the author of four books, two of them about Amelia Earhart. The first book, *Legerdemain*, was first self-published in 2005, then brought out in a second, enlarged edition through Saga Books in 2007. *Legerdemain* later placed as a finalist in the 2008 National Best Books competition under History: U.S. Nonfiction. In 2012, Dave published the coffee-table book *The Story of Amelia Earhart*, which has been very popular. His website address is www.davidkbowman.com, and he makes his home in Auburn, WA.

Made in the USA
Middletown, DE
19 September 2021